AF511940

SOCIAL ETHNOGRAPH
OF THE HILL MUSLIM
OF NEPAL

SOCIAL ETHNOGRAPHY OF THE HILL MUSLIMS OF NEPAL

Dr. PRAKASH UPADHYAY

ADROIT

Adroit Publishers
New Delhi

Published by

ADROIT PUBLISHERS

4675/21, Ganpati Bhawan, Ansari Road,

Daryaganj, New Delhi-110 002

Phone : 011-23266030

email: adroitpublishers@gmail.com

Distributors

AKHIL BOOK DISTRIBUTORS

email: akhilbooks@yahoo.com

akhilbks@gmail.com

© Dr. PRAKASH UPADHYAY

© Author, 2014

No part of this publication may be reproduced or transmitted in any form or by any means, electronic or mechanical, including photocopying, recording or any information storage and retrieval system, without permission in writing from the publisher & author.

Requests for permission to make copies of any part of the work should be mailed to:

Copyrights & Permissions Department

ADROIT PUBLISHERS

ISBN : 978-81-87393-06-1

Printed in India on behalf of M/s Adroit Publishers by

Akhil Sharma, E-mail: adroitpublishers@gmail.com

PREFACE

Among the socially excluded religious minority groups in Nepal, hill Muslim community is one of the communities where there is high level of paucity, low level of education and health indicators. Similarly, they have very low access in productive resources and national policy and governance structures. Among multiple challenges, one of the challenges for them is to preserve the culture, traditions and language of the community and increase their access in all levels of national governance structures. The superstitious values and religious dogma restricting family planning, the demands on Muslim women to reproduce children due to the high social value of children and the way the procreation of children is built into the political and economic systems of society, has created various complications. *The strict Islamic religious credo and century's old social exclusions have created a dilemma of poverty amidst plenty of human and natural resources. Owing to this the Muslim masses are unable to fulfill their basic needs easily and are unable to break away from fatalism and culture of poverty cycle. The lack of adequate inclusion of Muslims in institutional stake has helped uphold the gap between people, the institutions and mainstream society. Poverty and vulnerability has continued to transmit through generations. Accordingly the hopes of transformation has been restrained under the sadistic cycle of social-economic chauvinism, failure to raise social-economic status has led to segregation from the mainstream society, and a stipulation of pauperization is emerging, preparing a ground for the conversion of Muslims into waged laborers (proletariat) under a brisk process of proletariatisation despite their mass migration for jobs in gulf countries. This is ultimately costing high for the whole Nepali society—Muslims loosing interest in legal and Nepalese administrative systems, health/education etc and is aiding in preparing the ground for the rise of Islamic fundamentalism in the hills of Nepal.*

This book calls for understanding the magnitude of the process of social inclusion and responding to Nepal's diversity by carrying out an examination through the lens of social inclusion, ethnicity/caste, religion, and regional identity. This will potentially help in understanding the sentiments of the religious minority groups which will consequently reduce the possible tensions and ethno-religious conflicts in South-Asia.

Dr. Prakash Upadhyay

Associate Professor of Anthropology,

Tribhuvan University, Nepal

January 2014

CONTENT

1

INTRODUCTION

A Succinct History of Nepal

Nepal with its conserved grandeur of being independent and sovereign throughout history, has witnessed various notable political movements, the last in 2006 which was a spontaneous republican revolution against the totalitarianism of autocratic monarch. The aftermath of republic is also not gratis of predicaments which are evident from uprisings in Terai region, tumult in hilly and mid-hill regions, and demand of ethnic and religious minorities for *adequate representation with identity* in all spheres of the nation that led consequently to the debacle and demise of first constituent assembly in 2012.

Liberal political environment, globalization, urbanization and migration amid the hectic political process of constitution drafting trapped in the issue of federalism and inclusion made the issue of religion and ethnicity more debatable in Nepal. New ethnic identities were forged, new religious and ethnic associations set up, and new allegations made in social, political, religious, geographical and economic sectors for the reorganization of the country. In the past, ethnicity and religion never became a prominent issue in the politics of Nepal. This was particularly the case during the party-less Panchayati era (1960-1990), during which a sturdy emphasis was put on the undesirability of religious and ethnic politics as part of the efforts to consolidate national identity and unity. The Panchayati slogan *ek desh, ek bhesh, ek bhasa* (one country, one dress, and one language) proved perilous to Terai people and to many ethnic and religious minority groups. The slogan one dress, one language tried to design a new united Nepali identity with a common dress *Daura-Suruwal-Dhaka Topi* (Nepali trouser and Nepali cap) and one language (Nepali language) excluding all others, but failed despicably to give equal caste/ethnic/religion/region based egalitarianism to all Nepali masses. After the people's revolution in 2006 and the consequent establishment of republican set-up in 2008, both forms of identity (ethnicity and religion based) seemed to come increasingly to the forefront, and accusations of ethnic or religious bias are today commonly voiced in the political discourse of the country. Although this logic seems lucrative politically, but there are dangers of defining exclusion only in terms of caste, ethnicity and religion. There are high chances of politicization of ethnicity and religion charm.

The internal politics of Nepal is not free of interferences. Delimited by the giant communist China to the north and democratic India to the east, west and south, Nepal's political identity and status has been to a great extent influenced by Indian, Chinese and Western foreign policy interest in the internal affairs of Nepal. *Latent and manifest* interferences of vested interests are playing with their invisible hands in manipulating Nepali politics and society. The long established subsistence agriculture based semi-feudal totalitarian governments, social, cultural and political hypocrisy and feudalistic nature of governance in Nepal has given birth to a modern form of dependency (internal and external) based semi-feudalism which is preparing the ground for external interferences as well as internal social, cultural, economic and political tumult.

Until 1951, members of the autocratic feudalistic Rana oligarchy held complete control of the government in Nepal. In 1951, after a revolt led by the Political parties, autocratic Rana oligarchy came to an end but the residual of feudalism with political and dependency nexus endures even in 21st century which are accountable for quandaries and crisis. **Humans** are unique owing to caliber of their conscious awareness of themselves and their situation. They are capable of self – reflection and hence, assessment of their positions in society is possible through their self-consciousness (Marx, 1859). Such consciousness arises out of people's daily existence and is not a realm of ideas that is somehow independent of the material world of elites. In Nepal self-consciousness of masses and humanly may be the history, a change from feudalistic age to multiparty republican democracy after the people's movements in different time phases, high elite culture and elitism still dominates urban as well rural Nepal which is a reminisce of feudalism partly in semi feudalistic vicious cycle operated by political elites. The term *elite* itself is confusing and resilient with various meanings, depending upon the type of establishment, semi-feudal society, agro-based economy, culture and change.

The social world around is a materialization of man's praxis; his prolific activity in history is not just an assertion that nature is man made. Man's understanding of the material world is a reflection of his own social world and the history of existing societies has been the history of an assortment of struggles. In the words of Marx (1859) 'free man and slave, patrician and plebian, lord and serf, guild master and Journey man in a word, oppressor and oppressed, stood in constant apposition to one another, carried on an uninterrupted, now hidden, now open fight that each time ended either in a revolutionary reconstruction of society at large with the annihilation of *elitism* or in the common ruin of contending classes'. The long history of totalitarian governments and feudalistic nature of governance in Nepal has been challenged many times by the masses. But the upholding process of semi-feudalism thrived. Throughout its history, there has been the existence of various types of ruling elites, political elites or elites of different kinds in the social and economic strata of Nepalese society that helped to dilute the common people's frustration against totalitarianism and suppressions.

Since 2008, Nepal is a *Republic* but the country has been fundamentally governed by the ruling elites throughout its history. Before the Rana regime (1768-1846 AD), few elite families such as the Thapa, Basnyat and Pandey ruled Nepal under the banner of Shah Kings. During Rana regime (1846-1950 AD), members of the autocratic feudalistic familial oligarchy of Rana family held complete control of the government in Nepal. After the end of Rana oligarchy in 1951 first free elections were held in 1959 and a new constitution introduced, however, in December 1960 King Mahendra banned all political parties and suspended the constitution. In 1962, a new constitution was drafted which set up a party-less Panchayati government and party-less council known as the *Rashtriya Panchayat* with king as the autocratic executive head of the elite government. Few elite families who were in proximity to *Narayanhiti* Royal Palace ruled Nepal, took advantage and emerged as neo-elites. In the long trot they became politically powerful elites and a sharp polarization between them and the common masses transpired. Owing to the high concentration of elites in Kathmandu, there resulted in regional bias in development, the high development of Kathmandu and core urban areas and the underdevelopment and marginalization of secluded regions and the people. The underdevelopment and marginalization of common masses prepared the ground for the emergence of Nepali society as one of the most unequal societies on earth. It also led to the outburst of peoples frustrations in various forms in different time phases. The political ambitions in nexus with grievances and frustrations of people were visible during nineteen days glorious political movement of the Nepali people in 2006 and the Terai uprising in 2007. However, the aftermath of movements witnessed people's strong sentiments, high ambitions and demand for more inclusiveness, more regional autonomy, and end of historical legacy of social, political, economic inequalities/hegemony. Amidst a vicious cycle of crisis, the current crisis (social, cultural, economic, political) in Nepal is explainable on the base of a set of hypotheses about social/cultural, ethnic, regional, economic, religious and political relations especially about a demand for more autonomy, social/cultural, ethnic, regional, economic, religious, political rights and inclusiveness, development and more speedy changes.

Predicaments: A Historical-Theoretical Perusal

Conflict perspective embedded with Marxist Anthropology developed in response to discontent with numerous facets of contemporary anthropological theory. Most notably, perhaps, Marxist anthropology questioned the validity of treating small-scale societies as isolated, suspended in time and space, rather than as elements in colonial and postcolonial world. Marxist anthropology also presented itself in a quite different way as it questioned both *functionalists tendency* to attribute equal force to all elements in the social system, and the *Structuralists* claims that social life was driven by the structure of people's thought rather than the practical outcome of their actions. Structural Marxists sought after a compromise position, arguing that the material conditions of existence cannot completely determine people's ideas and that people's ideas (consciousness) are determined by their entrenchment with a mode of production, but stick on to the enlightenment principle that the detached observer is exempt and can objectively determine the true causes of events. However, it rejects the converse proposition, that people's ideas can have a determinative effect on their material or social condition. Marxist argument is that the quintessence of people's lives is the process of production since for Marx, human life involves before anything else eating and drinking, a habitation, clothing, and many other material things. To meet these necessities of life, production is necessary, but as production satisfies one set of needs, new needs arise and encourage alterations in the ways that productive activity is organized. The elaboration of productive activity creates a division of labor, which, in the end, is alienating because it increasingly deprives human of their capacity to determine their productive activities and supports the elites. Historically, the disproportionate division of labour and resources between common Nepalese and the elites created acute alienation between these two groups in Nepal. It involved processes vigorously restructuring the material conditions of Nepalese people's existence and in the process predicaments transpired in the course of demand for more economic rights, political, social, ethnic and other rights on the part of common people living in different parts of the country.

In the analysis of class structure, several early Marxist argued that Marx's scheme had to be revisited because there was no real sign of heightened class struggle. Amid the declining poverty owing to foreign remittance generated by Nepalese laborers working abroad, Nepal has however, seen instances of heightened class struggle between *haves (rich)* and *have not (poor)*. The widening gap between neo-rich people (neo-elites) and the worsening class status of common masses, massive unemployment, economic sluggishness and political instability in Nepal can be explained in an attempt to adapt the basic situation of a necessary conflict between labor and capital as well as between vested interests and prevailing feudalistic attitude. Changes can be traced in Nepal in the patterns of property ownerships, changes in relationships at work, class divisions, and rise of elitism and side by side growth of more conscious urban based middle class also, exploitation, growing unrests, unemployment, migration for foreign labour and internal conflicts. However, it is practically unfeasible to comprehend and solve the problems related to social unrests and anarchy in the absence of a proper mechanism explaining the relationship between the growing elitism with its historical legacy and the scramble for social inclusion, more autonomy, and social/cultural, economic and political rights on the part of common people.

Correlations

Establishing the correlation between current social, economic and political crises and the conflict standpoint, it is evident that Nepalese economy has taken the form of distinguishing different capital fractions and of providing an account of the monopoly phase of political, economic and cultural privileged. How differences of power develop when elitism is institutionalized and the sharing of productive resources is discriminated to commoners is the issue of special inquiry. Coser (1964) argues that conflicts have some social functions and implications, which ought to be seen at – the levels of conflicting parts and at the system as a whole. However, the growing unrest in different parts of Nepal, political and economic crises and incidents aftermath makes it clear that although conflicts may have functions in bringing different changes, however when more unequal is the distribution of scarce resources; the greater is the conflict of interest between dominant and subordinate segments in a system. The more subordinate segments become aware of their true collective interests, the more likely are they to question the legitimacy of the existing pattern of distribution of scarce resources. The more social changes brought by dominant segments disrupt the existing relations among subordinates; the more likely are the masses to become aware of their true interest. If the common people become responsive of their cooperative interests and the bigger is their questioning of the validity of the distribution of political power, political actions and scarce resources, the more likely they are to join blatant struggle against dominant privileged segments of a system. In Nepal midst incongruities, the student's movement and the consequent referendum of 1980 provided people a choice between a reformed version of the existing party-less Panchayati system or a multiparty based system, which resulted in the return of the existing party-less Panchayati system amidst election manipulation and mass misuse of state machinery by the than royal government. In June 1985 an underground extremist group launched a bombing campaign against monarchy in which many people were killed. The state arrested thousands of opposition supporters. In 1989, Nepal's relation with India became tense when Indian government imposed an economic blockage over a dispute regarding 1950 ***Special Relationship Treaty.*** The fall of Berlin Wall and East European Communist regimes, visit of Indian political leaders Chandrasekhar, Harkishan Singh Surjeet in February 1990 to express Indian solidarity to Nepalese political parties, primed the ground for the coalition of Nepalese political parties (who were never united in the past) and demand for the restoration of multi-party democracy in Nepal. The successful movement in 1990 led to the termination of the party less autocratic rules of the monarch and the formation of an interim all party government in Nepal to draft a constitution and to conduct multiparty election. The interim government promulgated a new democratic constitution in 1990.

However, democratic period in Nepal remained embedded in uneasiness since the elections of 1991. Since 1991 to 2013, Nepal saw an assortment of forms of government (single to jumbo coalitions), political malfunctions, uprising of Maoist insurgents, people's popular Movement part-II, election of constituent assembly and its failure to draft a new constitution, social and economic anarchism and the political instability that jeopardized the country. This led to augment of frustration for politics and democracy in Nepal. Democracy proved to be a corrupt practice in Nepal. Even in modern democratic republican age, poor Nepali people are not the real beneficiaries in development projects and the elites living on the top have always remained the true beneficiaries of all development models. The structure of Nepali society and culture in essence, is strictly built hierarchical and intrinsically built –in with the values and principles of ambiguities and contradictions in everyday speech and work and because of these perpetuating cultural values, the Nepalese democracy has not been able to cross the barriers of *family, caste* and *kinship* and consequently leading towards *inaction* and unrests in every aspect of the society. It is necessary that policy makers and foreign donor agencies comprehend that Nepali society is pluralistic society and a homogenous model of development may or may not work. It is a mordant authenticity that even after all political exercises, the governance system remained the reflection of the past legacy; the old traditional elites still occupy key positions in every institution all over the country. The same traditional domineering elitist structure based on family and kinship nepotism operates and the bottom-up process of democratic politics remained a distant dream still in Nepal. Real Democracy remained *part time* –democracy only for few elites and caste and religious groups. The grassroots democracy stands only *rhetoric and a delusion for majority*.

The ruling monarch Birendra Shah and his whole family were massacred in 2001. There led to ascend of new political power paradigm in the political horizon of Nepal after this incident. This was a paradigm shift in apathy to political parties who were involved in diverse sorts of malfunctioning. It weakened the democratic forces and institutions in Nepal and to great extent political parties were responsible for the weakening position of democratic institutions. The new king Gyanendra Shah grabbing the opportunity of weakening political parties dismissed the government of Prime Minister Sher Bahadur Deuba for the second time and took over executive power in his hand in January 2005 and declared emergency. It was an overt royal coup d'état. During the mid of festivals season in October 2005, the autocratic monarch's government brought much criticized Media Ordinance, in the words of Information ministry to regulate the media sector of Nepal. However, the civil society and parties severely criticized the ordinance and appealed the international community to oppose the ordinance. The Office of the UN High Commissioner for Human Rights (OHCHR) in Nepal asserted that the new media ordinance violated international human rights standards and it lacked respect for the rule of law in Nepal. The seizure of broadcasting equipments from radio stations and a large deployment of armed police raised serious issues regarding respect for the rule of law and reverence for freedom of expression in Nepal. OHCHR said that it regard media ordinance restrictions too broad, ambiguously worded, and sufficiently focused on a specific threat. US Senator Tom Daschle who visited Nepal in July 2005 criticized the ordinance and termed as dangerous the steps taken by government to muzzle independent media.

Human rights violations under the rule of autocratic monarch, political deadlocks, Maoist uprising, development stalemate, International diplomacies and situations, political and economic misuses paved the mode for people's historic heroic movement in 2006 which was a sort of *mutiny* against elitism- the monarch's exclusiveness and autocracy. The Narayanhiti Royal Palace massacre that obliterated the whole family of king Birendra in 2001, ostracized activities of new king Gyanendra Shah and crown prince Paras Shah brought Nepal on the threshold of corrosion with a new political polarization and a political paradigm shift against the king. Seven parliamentarian political parties signed 12 point concord with the then banned Maoist militia in late 2005 and this prepared the ground for a paradigm shift from constitutional monarchy to *Loktantric* (democratic) People's Republic. The monarch in 2006 overlooked the political paradigm shift and mass sentiments, and announced local elections for municipalities on February 8, 2006. Elections were conducted with a meager 19% voting. India and other democratic powers including USA and European Union refuted to give validity to the so called *drama election*. The Maoist insurgents by the time were engaged in waging war against the State from jungle and were claiming that 70% of rural Nepal was under their control. Political parties declared so called elections *futile* and actively boycotted the polls. Parties also provided the top alliance leaders the mandate to continue further talks with the Maoist insurgents which paved the ground for another political paradigm shift- *a new paradigm shift integrating seven parliamentary parties with Maoist.* This paradigm shift was an alliance to autocratic and dictatorial rule of the king and dissatisfactions with several aspects of contemporary political and economic events. Most importantly, political parties, common people and civil society questioned the rising social, economic and political unrests and also the validity of treating political parties as isolated from the people by the autocratic monarch and his eccentric son crown prince Paras Shah through dictatorial means and the policy of *divide and rule*. The autocratic monarch's operation pattern was suspended in time and space, rather than as elements working for the welfare of the people. Haunted by the fantasy of Narayanhiti *Palace ghost* Nepalese people ultimately actively challenged the dictatorial rule of monarch. A nineteen days people's gallant movement and the martyrdom of more than two dozens lives, mutilation of thousands compelled the autocratic monarch to surrender before the people and to hand over power to political parties. People's annoyance had developed in response to dissatisfactions with several aspects of contemporary political events, consequently paving the way for People's movement part--II in April 2006 that led to the downfall of monarch and the rise of *Loktantrik Ganatantra (Democratic Republic)*. Most significantly, common people, political parties and civil society questioned the validity of monarchy which was isolated from the people, was suspended in time and space, and was working as an institution working for the interests of the rulers and elites rather than the common masses. Common Nepalese also questioned the tendency of unjustified splitting up and use of power between Political parties, Palace, and Military in the political system. They also reckon that political parties are functioning on of their own political vested interest rather than thinking about people's grievances, and drafting new constitution.

Asymmetrical distribution of scarce resources in favor of few, concentration of scarce resources in elite hands especially elite upper caste Hindus, social exclusion of religious and ethnic minorities, political variances and semi-feudalistic exploitations lead to the augmentation of common Nepalese's frustration that led to the downfall of Monarchy. Analogous to French Revolution and aftermath of 1789, in Nepal, in the upshot of the political change of 2006 and owing to the lack of proper governance, impunity and control mechanism on the part of political parties and government, reluctance and lack of vision to draft new constitution, to dispatch autonomy and more power to common masses, escorted to more political and social unrests, strikes, violence and misdemeanor and when politicized got a political color in the form of political violence in Terai and other regions in the hills and urban areas of Nepal. The hidden sentiments and the grievances of diverse ethnic and religious minorities were ignited by the vested interests of politicians. The grievances of ethnic minorities residing in different parts of Nepal got a momentum. The issue of social exclusion of religious minority Muslims got a thrust. The issues of Muslims emerged at an optimum boiling point.

Muslims and the Prevailing Stipulations

Ethnography is a holistic study covering the history, analysis of the topographical conditions- geographical diversities, the climate, terrain, the habitat and the culture as a whole. As it is reflective, it hence makes a substantial contribution toward the understanding of the social life of humans, having an artistic impact on the reader and express convincing reality. Ethnography observes the people from the perspective of view of the subject with a total observation of people's behavior with a description of all symbol-meaning relations using concepts that avoid casual explanations. Social ethnography deals with orientations, or behaviors, social constructivism, social psychology and social capital that take into account the interests, intentions, or need of the people. The social psychology, social capital, ethno-linguistic and religious composition of the population of South Asia is appallingly diverse. The majority of the populations are socially, culturally and psychologically diverse. They fall within four large linguistic family groups, Indo-Aryan, Tibeto-Burman, Austro-Asiatic and Dravidian. These groups are further subdivided into numerous sub-groups, castes and tribes however Indo-Aryans form the largest ethno-linguistic group not only in Nepal but also in North India, Bangladesh, Pakistan, Sri Lanka and the Maldives. The major religions of the region are Hinduism, Islam, Christianity, Buddhism, Sikhism, Jainism and many other minor religions. Hindu religion remains socially, culturally and politically dominant religion in Nepal owing to which minority groups has been excluded incessantly in this country. However, historically, Nepal has been constantly portrayed as demonstrating *unity in diversity*, an ethnic and cultural mosaic exemplifying cultural plurality. **Prithvi Narayan Shah, the founder of modern Nepal in 1768 had declared that *Nepal is a garden of the four Varna (castes) and thirty-six Jat* (ethnicities). This is a phrase which has been endlessly repeated in the modern period.**

For thousands of years, Nepal has served as a brand of shelter for various religions, cultures, and ethnic groups. The Aryans who entered Nepal from India became the originator and profounder of Hindu religion by developing a unique harmonious but hegemonic relationship with ethnic and minority groups. There are probably few other places in the world which have such a high level of cultural diversity within a small territory. Theoretically, there is high level of unity and consensus prevailing among the caste/ethnic people but in practice this unity and consensus is based on the hegemony of the dominant group on minorities. The nineteenth century *Old Legal Code* of Nepal (called *Muluki Ain* in Nepali) determined the hierarchy of different caste/ethnic groups till mid 20th century. Despite the stratification of caste/ethnic groups, the Muluki Ain and especially the process of Sanskritization, assisted in strengthening the social structure of Nepali society. The Muluki Ain assembled the diverse caste/ethnic groups under the Hindu caste system called *Varnashram* in Sanskrit language and had done further categorization. In case of wrong doings and crimes, punishments were announced on the basis of their caste hierarchy. Hypergamy created the opportunities for the low caste women to be promoted to the upper position through her marriage with high caste male. Caste became the feature of Nepali society and *isogamy* stood as the major feature of caste system. Isogamy was endorsed in Brahmin society and it helped in maintaining their status. Isogamy, Endogamy and Hypergamy become the part of Nepali caste system and were enforced and strengthened by Muluki Ain. This long established tradition helped in the creation of a strict Hindu social structure in Nepal that is made up of different institutions. In the process caste/ethnities became the constituent made up from different peoples from different background. Sanskritization created the opportunity for hypergamy which was blocked by *isogamy* and this was done to strengthen the social and familial bond that reflects the basic norms of functionalism. The assimilation of different ethnic groups especially in the hills ***helped in stabilizing the Hindu society. Hindu*** religion facilitated a lot in stabilizing the diverse communities especially in creating a unique syncretism between Hinduism and Buddhism. This has created such a condition that both Hindus and Buddhists people worship each others deities and follow each others rituals and this has been possible due the amalgamation of different groups owing to Sanskritization and Hinduization process. The unique tradition in Nepal has been such that different caste/ethnic groups worship the same deities, speak the same language, and have similar social organizations. Indeed, they became the part of the broader Nepali society. Different festivals, ceremonies and processions are observed by the both Hindus and Buddhists. People from both religions actively participate in processions and festivals and the festivals and feasts played a vital role in unifying and integrating the Nepali society. However, this process of unification excluded other minority religions and groups especially Islam which has been historically regarded as an alien religion in this country. Even after the establishment of democracy in 1951, the national census data ignored the number of ethnic and religious minorities. In fact, the size of various ethnic/caste groups in the total population was hardly known before 1990 despite Nepal being a multiethnic, multilingual and multicultural country. The eleventh census of 2011, for the first time, identified more than 125 ethnic/caste groups and more than 123 languages in multiethnic Nepal. The total population stands at 26,494,505 (The Central Bureau of Statistics, 2011). By 2011, the multi-ethnic and multi-religious population of Nepal has grown to 1.35%, since the last census in 2001. The male population stands at 12,849,041 while population of female is 13,645,463. The sex ratio is 94.16 compared to 99.8 of 2001 census. Terai region constitutes 50.27 percent (13,318,705) of the total population. Similarly, hilly and mountain areas constitute 43 percent (11,394,007) and 6.73 percent (1,781,792) respectively. The census data also show that more than half of the population, about 55 per cent, is below 25 years of age in Nepal.

Despite social, cultural, ethnic and religious diversities, even at the present in the 21st century, under the parasol of Republican democratic political system, Nepal failed to include the marginalized backwards groups like the Muslim, Women, low caste groups called Dalits, indigenous nationalities, people of Nepal Terai region called *Madhesis*, in the mainstream of the nation. These ill-fated people have been constantly been debarred from mainstream development historically, politically, socially and economically. A long history of the continuation of political autocracy, social exclusion, marginalization and exclusion from access to resources, services and opportunities, disempowerment, cultural and ritual debasement, discrimination and marginalization (on the basis of religious affiliation, caste, ethnicity, culture, language, territorial/geographical origin/remoteness and gender, and capacity constraints) are the major impediments for the inclusion of diverse ethnic and caste groups in the national development efforts. Most of the achievements and resources through the past development process has gone to governing caste and ethnic groups, however, the issue of ethnicity in Nepal is exclusive and dissimilar from other countries. The diffident subordinate groups which came to be created slowly in Nepal were not due to colonialism or voluntary or involuntary migration (as in United States) or annexation but were created slowly by internal processes that consequently deliberately resulted in the constrained access to resources, services and opportunities, disempowerment, cultural and ritual debasement, discrimination and marginalization on the basis of religious affiliation, caste, ethnicity, culture, language, territorial/geographical origin/remoteness and gender, and capacity constraints as the major forms of segregation that different marginalized social groups are facing today. The social, economic and political segregations in different forms with a historical legacy continues to be a major hindrance in Nepal's development owing to which most of the achievements through past development process has gone to governing caste and ethnic groups.

The diffident subordinate ethnic and religious groups which came to be created slowly in Nepal were not due to colonialism or voluntary or involuntary migration (as in United States) or annexation but were created slowly by internal processes in the majority of cases. Unlike in the United States of America, in Nepal, *race* has never been perceived as a category no matter how strongly one has a tendency to find it. Except for those who came to Nepal during the last hundred years or so from the adjoining territories, Nepalese of all ethnicity may fairly be described as native people from different races like Mongoloid, Aryans, Dravidian etc. Race is connected to the cataloging of human bodies that are considered similar in certain ways. The creed of race evolved from the perception that there were innate biological differences between people of different skin colors and places, that- indeed- there were no ancestors common to all of humanity whereas ethnicity has to do with culture, a group of people with shared languages, meanings, foods, beliefs, religion, customs, traditions, etc. On the contrary, ethnicity is not just a person's race; it is about institutions, learned behavior and customs. It is about where anyone comes from, and celebrating the traditions and ideas that are part of that region. It has opportunity to change because groups can reject their own and embrace another in a process of assimilation. For example, the Sanskritization process of Nepal and India before 1950 converted many ethnic and non-Hindu religious groups to Hindu religion and Hindu life styles. Although there are numerous negative insinuations for the subordinate group status of numerous ethnic groups in Nepal, the consequences are not as severe as those faced by blacks in the United States of America, or Nazi Germany's Jews before 1945. In Nepal, the subordinate groups were never compelled by the dominant groups to leave the habitat or evacuate the country. This tendency of domination lacks evidences of heinous racial crimes as committed in the United States of America during the nineteenth century and even up to the mid 20th century. Religious minorities of Nepal were never driven out of the country as in the cases of Pakistan, Bangladesh or the former Yugoslovakia.

Contrary to ethnicity, the word 'Indigenous' is a term quite different. Indigenous peoples are the original stewards of the environment or the *Bhumiputra* (son of the land), holding the land of their ancestors in trust for future generations. They have no history of migration from other places. They are those distinct and vulnerable *tribes* who possess only a limited ability to participate in, and are most often marginalized by the development process. They previously may have (or not) have long-term experience of self-governance. The original meaning of the term 'indigenous' is inborn that originates from a locality, those who uphold a combined identity through association with specific territories. Tribal, indigenous, ethnic minority, hunter/gatherer, etc. are used as analogous appellations, but meanings vary considerably depending on who sets the boundaries. A growing conflict exists between the supporters of the newly-emerging UN criteria for indigenousness and the over and over again unrealistic requirements demanded by certain non-native elites, particularly in Africa and Asia. In Nepal, there is flawed understanding on the definition of Indigenous groups. If hunting and gathering is the criteria for being called an indigenous group, are *Raute* (Stone Age people still living in caves) the indigenous group of Nepal? Nepalese history reveals that about all the groups living in Nepal are the migrants from North, South, East or West. It signifies that the identification of indigenous peoples is blurry in Nepal. The migrants also brought their popular religions along with them. For example Hinduism was introduced thousands of years back by the Aryans coming from North India. Similarly Islam was introduced in Nepal by different Muslim groups who entered Nepal in different time phases.

There are minority religious groups with their distinct religions, cultural traditions and beliefs and the legacy of subordination has created a sadistic situation in Nepal owing to which among the excluded subordinated groups, there is comparatively high level of poverty and low level of development indicators - economic, education, health. They have comparatively very low access in productive resources, national policy and governance structures. Among multiple challenges, one of the challenges for them is to preserve their religion, ethnic cultures, languages and traditions and progress ahead amid ethnic stereotypes in a volatile democracy. The ethnic stereotype **prevailing in Nepali society is the crux which** is a simplified and often misleading representation of religious and ethnic groups' history and origin, composed of what are thought to be typical characteristics of members of religious and ethnic groups.

Among the excluded marginalized minority groups, Muslim community living in both Terai and hill is one of the communities where there is high level of poverty and low level of education and health indicators. Similarly, they have very low access in productive resources and national policy and governance structures. Among multiple challenges, one of the challenges for them is to preserve the culture, traditions and language of the community and increase their access in all levels of national governance structures (NPC, 2008). The superstitious values and religious dogma restricting family planning, the pressure on Muslim women to produce children is due to the high social value of children and the way the production of children is built into the political, economic and systems of society (Mathur, 1996). The status of a *religious alien* in a predominant Hindu dominated state has to a great extent has been one of the determining factor behind the present degraded religious, social, political and economic status of Muslims in Nepal. The end of autocratic rules and establishment of different regimes in Nepal hardly made any change in their social and economic status and they (Muslims) remained in paucity and tribulations. The situation remained unchanged even after the establishment of democracy in 1990 and the declaration of the nation as a democratic republic in 2008. Their condition remained unaltered though according to the national census of Nepal 2011, the Muslim population in Nepal stands at 4.4 per cent (1,164,255) in a predominant Hindu state with a Hindu population of 81.3 percent. Islam is the third largest religious group of Nepal after Hinduism and Buddhism. The descendants of the Muslims settled in the hills still constitute only over 4% of the total Muslim population of Nepal. Rest 96 % is settled in Terai region mostly bordering North Indian states (CBS, 2011). The Muslim community living in hills survives amid problems of diverse sorts, struggling hard for their existence. Amid diminishing resources and social-economic status of being a *religious alien*, the hill Muslims condition in the hills of Nepal is abysmal. The tribulations are grim in remote rugged hills where the hill Muslims (known as *Churoute* in Nepal) are living for centuries surrounded by majority Hindus and Buddhist population, debarred from the management and decision making processes at the local administrative levels and even in openly practicing Islam. Such segregation in due course may cost high for the mainstream society if this religious minority develop apathy in State establishment and the major social-economic systems of the mainstream that may consequently widen the gap between minority people, institutions and the people of the mainstream society.

The Muslims indifference towards the mainstream society is a prime problem. The historical context of the strict implementation of Hindu philosophy based code and state negligence is one of the reasons behind the indifference of Muslim community and their apathy for inclusion in national mainstream. Nepal has been historically a unitary state ruled constantly by elite caste and class owing to which domestic colonization has been supercilious in many parts of the country. This has created various economic, social, cultural and religious challenges for Muslims minorities specially the hill Muslims due to their geographical location. This has also generated a sense of insecurity and alienation among them from the national mainstream. How far Muslim masses of Nepal would integrate in the national mainstream and join the nation building programme under a new political environment remains obscure but if the same gloomy condition prevails they will remain diffident lacking inclusion---*politically, socially, and economically*.

Not only the Muslims, the major bulk of Nepalese people live surrounded by paucity and countable people can have a contented life. Also an immense preponderance of the rural population in Nepal struggle decisively for an immense range of resources and services. This shapes and defines correlation of the people with their status i.e. the **Social-economic status** (SES) which is a combined measure of an individual's or family's economic and social position relative to others, based on income, education, and occupation. Social-economic status is typically broken into three categories, high SES, middle SES, and low SES to describe the three areas a family or an individual may fall into. When placing a family or individual into one of these categories any or all of the three variables (income, education, and occupation) are appraised and are the strong predictors related to available resources. In the context of Muslims, state apathy and exclusion ultimately is costing high for the society as they persevere to loose interest in institutions as legal systems, administrative systems, health/education etc under a sharp process of social-economic deterioration. The lack of adequate inclusion of these populations in mainstream institutional stake is helping maintain the gap between people and the institutions. Consequently, poverty and vulnerability is continuing to transmit through generations amid the availability of abundant man power and natural resources. Hence given the stipulation, in the perspective of hill Muslims (*Churoute*) it is imperative to grasp the prevailing *poverty or plenty* dichotomy embedded with social-economic and demographic characteristics in relation to available resources that will enable a reorientation in development paradigms and approaches that will hub focus on development needs of Muslim ethnic minority. It is to be realized that the *concept of social, economic and political adjustments* needs to be comprehended for a long lasting peace and democracy in the absence of which inclusive process of Nepali society, system and nation can't endure. It will be imperative to explore social exclusion, the prevailing social-economic and ethnographic stipulation of *Poverty vs. Plenty* dichotomies of the hill Muslims and to uncover the repercussions of dichotomies and the resultant tribulations. Some questions are imperative which are discussed here:

1. *Where are the hill Muslims (Churoute) from? When and why did they migrate to this area of Nepal and when?*
2. *What is the existing trend of social-economic and ethnographic stipulation and characteristics of hill Muslims of Nepal? And how they subsist and what are their livelihood patterns, religious conventions and effects on development?*
3. *How are development, political structure, state policies and apathy, ethnography embedded conventions and social/cultural structure in rural Nepal organized and what influences they wield over the hill Muslims traditions, social exclusions, renovations and development efforts?*

There is a total lack of ethnographic study of hill Muslims by using *anthropological ethnographic lenses* hence the discussions offered in the book will be helpful in planning and implementation of potential projects and improvement of the existing social-economic condition of hill Muslims in Nepal. Hub has been made on the prevailing situation of social exclusion and the dichotomies of social-economic status, issues and grievances that would be useful as a reference for the scholars, researchers, planners, and policy makers profoundly. Comprehension, revision and implementation of potential planning and projects in the long run possibly will support national unity and integration via the lofty inclusion of Muslims in national mainstream of Nepal and ensure enduring development and serenity in the whole region.

2

MUSLIMS HISTORY IN NEPAL: A THEORETICAL ANALYSIS

The Hindu Shah rulers of Nepal with their mighty swords ruthlessly ruled Nepal for 240 years starting from 1768 to 2008. Their system of governance was based on Hindu scriptures. As Buddhism was accepted as a part of Hindu religion and society, the followers of this religion had no problem in Nepal. But Muslims, the third religious group were allowed to practice their faith under certain restrictions. They were debarred from propagation of Islam or to follow the Islamic code *Shariat* in respect of dissolution of marital relationship by oral pronouncement of the word *Talaq* (marital separation/divorce) thrice. In case of inheritance also they were to follow the Hindu-scriptures based code of Nepal. A Hindu scripture based Nepal Code was the legal code and any violation was a punishable offence. The situation therefore, was not congenial for the Islamic community to settle in Nepal. Even during Mughal rule in India, Muslim migration to Nepal was insignificant. Perhaps strict implementation of Hindu scriptures based code was the main reason behind the indifference of the Muslim community towards settling in Nepal. Owing to such restrictions, Muslims faced diverse tribulations in the process of becoming a significant third religious group in Nepal amid the prevailing religious constraints and deeply rooted feudalism. Consequently, the study and scope of religio-political anthropology of the Muslims of South Asia which has been the hot subject for historians for over last many decades in South Asia, is found to be proportionately minimal in the Hindu religion dominated Nepal. Muslims have been always regarded as a *religious alien* in this country.

Historically, it is difficult to come to any definite conclusion on the issue of Muslim migration in Nepal, but it is believed that when the Muslim ruler Bakhtiyalr Khilji invaded Tibet in 13th century, some of his soldiers entered secretly into Nepal. It is also believed that first arrival of Muslims in Kathmandu valley was in late fifteenth and early sixteenth century during the reign of King Ratna Malla, when Kashmiri traders from Tibet came here via Tibet for their trade in carpets, rugs and woolen garments. Soon after them some bangle sellers locally known as *Churoute* also arrived in Kathmandu valley. It is also said that the rulers of Nepal invited a few dozens of Muslim army personnel from neighbouring Indian Territory to train the soldiers in fire arms. The Muslim rulers could not annex Nepal due to the fighting capability of Gurkhas. Shamsuddin Ilyas, Muslim ruler of Bengal raided the Kathmandu valley in 1349 but returned without success (Bista, 1967). The bravery and guerilla warfare capability of Gurkhas proved to be major barrier for the Muslim invaders to capture Nepal. The predominance of Hindu population in Nepal also discouraged the Muslim invaders to settle and claim a right in this country. Nevertheless, the Muslim arrival in Nepal continued slowly and steadily and in the long run Sunni Muslims become the dominant Muslim group in Nepal. However, Nepal's Muslims, while they are mainly Sunni, constitute a heterogeneous group. Their ancestors arrived in Nepal from different parts of South Asia and Tibet during different epochs, and have since lived peacefully amidst the numerically dominant Hindus.

Kashmiri Muslims who arrived in Kathmandu valley during the reign of Malla dynasty King Ratna Malla (1484-1520 AD) built a mosque, the Kashmiri Takia, and engaged in different occupations—as scribes to correspond with the Delhi Sultanate, and as perfume manufacturers, musicians and bangle suppliers. Some were admitted as courtiers to the Malla palaces, and many traded with Tibet .The descendants of these migrants live in Kathmandu even to these days and they are called Muslims of Kathmandu valley. The second group of Muslims to enter the Kathmandu Valley was those of Hindustani origin. This group arrived during the reign of another Malla dynasty king Pratap Malla (1641-1674), who allowed them to put up a separate mosque in the southern part of the property belonging to the Kashmiri Takia. This Hindustani mosque, now known as the Nepali *Jame Masjid*, is originally said to have been a Shia mosque. It was converted into a Sunni mosque by Maulana Sargaraz Shah, a relative of the last Mughal Emperor of India Bahadur Shah Zafar, who arrived with the followers of Begum Hazrat Mahal of Lucknow when she took shelter in Kathmandu after the suppression of the Indian soldiers Mutiny by the British East India Company in 1857.

In the historical milieu the third group of Muslims to settle in Nepal came from different parts of northern India during the 16th and 17th centuries, invited by hill rulers to manufacture military armament (including traditional tanks with explosives). They remained in the hills also as makers of agricultural implements, utensils and ornaments. Though the descendants of these migrants are known as the hill Muslims or *Churoute*, or bangle-sellers, a majority survived as farmers. It is to be noted that in Nepali language bangle is called *Chura*; hence as bangle sellers, Muslims were called *Churoute*. There is a fair smidgen of these hill Muslims in Nepal's central and western hill districts of Tanahu, Gorkha, Kaski, Syangja, Palpa, Argakhanchi, Pyuthan and Dailekh. The Muslims residing in Terai region of Nepal arrived lately in the 20th century from North Indian states of Bihar and Uttar Pradesh as agriculture laborers or as migrants looking for fertile agricultural land.

There have been Muslim migrants of other origins also. Muslim migrants of Tibetan origin include both *Ladakhis* and those from Tibet proper. The latter arrived mostly after the Chinese takeover of Tibet in 1959, and in their language and dress these Tibetan Muslims are indistinguishable from their Tibetan Buddhist counterparts. Today, many are engaged in the trade of Chinese consumer durables and selling curios in different cities of Nepal. On the whole, this group tends to be more affluent economically than the other Muslim communities. While the smaller groups provide diversity, the largest community of Islam adherents—more than 95 percent—are the Muslims of the Terai. Concentrated in the Terai districts of Banke, Kapilvastu, Rupandehi, Parsa, Bara and Rauthat, some of the Terai Muslims were present here at the time of Nepal's unification in 1768 while others migrated from British India from the 19th century onwards as wage laborers. While most are small-time proprietor farmers, a substantial number still work as tenants and agricultural laborers. Here they do not speak Urdu, but Awadhi and Bhojpuri depending on whether they are of the Western or Central Terai.

The hill Muslims (*Churoute*) have been greatly influenced by the Hindu hill milieu nevertheless they follow Muslim rituals. But some Muslim practices like bride price and *Zakat* (charity collected during religious festivals) are irregularly observed by hill Muslims. The daily *Namaz* and month-long fasting during Ramadan are lightly dispensed by hill Muslims. In their dress, food habits and many of the customs are similar to Hindu neighbors. Living in the rugged hills of Nepali state for a very long period of time and sharing common historical experiences, hill Muslim groups have developed a stronger identification with the Nepali state. The Terai Muslims, on the other hand, like other Terai communities, continue to have strong ties -across the border and receive cultural sustenance from the larger Muslim population of Uttar Pradesh and Bihar state of India. Even though the fissure between the hill and the Terai Muslims has been wide, however, some of it is being bridged as educated Terai Muslims marry into Kathmandu's Kashmiri Muslim families, and *Moulavis* (Muslim priests) from the Terai take to visiting hill *madrassas* (Muslim School).

Other two groups of Muslims also sneaked into Nepal. These are the Bangladeshi (Bihari) refugees, who arrived in 1971 after the Indo-Pak war, most of whom have been repatriated to Pakistan. Likewise, there are the Kashmiri merchants who first arrived in the 1970s to set up curio shops in Kathmandu's tourist quarters. There has been a squirt in arrivals from Capital city of Indian Kashmir (Srinagar) since the political turmoil and militants insurgency escalated in Jammu and Kashmir of India in 1990. Many shopkeepers arrived with their stocks of woolen goods, handicrafts, rugs and furs. These recent arrivals have little or no interaction with the older Muslim residents, and most do not even know that there is an age-old Kashmiri Muslim population of 15th century in Indra-Chowk and other areas of Kathmandu valley.

During and after Sepoy mutiny of India in 1857 against the rule of British East India Company, there was a major penetration of Muslims in Terai region of Nepal. Jung Bahadur Rana, the first Rana Prime Minister of Nepal who was a close ally to British, gave protection and shelter to the Begum of Oudh. This was not possible without the consent of the British. It was a deliberate political move of the British to keep away the Muslim ruling family from its Indian Territory to avoid any mobilisation of Muslim masses around it. Knowing about the migration of the Begum of Oudh, the Muslims from the border area also started migrating to the Terai region of

Nepal. They were mostly farm laborers and small traders who were forced to flee to the Terai region of Nepal due to the British atrocities in the Ganges region. They entered Nepal as refugees to save their lives. The Hindu landlords were in need of the farm labor for cultivation and the rulers of the kingdom interested for more revenue from agricultural produce, placed no restriction for such migration of the Muslims as agricultural laborers. However, there was no relaxation in religious freedom for the migrant Muslims.

Although Muslim conquest of northern India had undermined the centuries old rigid anti-Muslim policy in the kingdom of Nepal to some extent, the sliding decline of Mughal Empire prompted successive rulers of Kathmandu valley to maintain its Hindu character. The founder of modern Nepal, Prithvi Narayan Shah during his regime (1743-1775) unified various independent hill kingdoms into modern Nepal. A few months before his death in 1775 he recorded the *'Divya Sandesh'* (King's so-called Divine message), which was a part of the guiding principles for state administration throughout the monarchial era. In his divine message he had envisaged Nepal as a holy land of Hindus- a real Hindustan for Hindus, contrasting with *Mughlana* (India), the land polluted by the rule of the Muslims of *Mughal* dynastry and their successors. This contemptuous language about India because of Muslim-rule over it remained a permanent mental load of Nepali masses. India was known as *Mughlana* as a common language of Nepalese. The people of Nepal made it a custom not to drive out the cow, the national animal from their field in south direction to stop its entry in *Mughlana*, where there was no state restriction on cow-slaughter (Helpton, 2005).

Jang Bahadur, the first Rana Prime Minister in the kingdom expanded the *'Divya Sandesh'* and framed 'Mulki Ain' *(National Legal Code/Law of the Land)* 1853 for strict implementation of the caste order based on Hindu social code, which listed the Muslims in the category of polluted and untouchables. The people of Nepal tolerated the Muslims known as *'Mlechchhas'* (barbarians) with restrictions to the extent that only "raw and dry eatables" were acceptable from their hands (Gaborieau, 2001). The Hindus were restricted from eating the animals slaughtered by Muslims. The traditional Nepali laws imposed various restrictions on Muslims. The Muslims of Nepal were compelled to strictly follow the Nepal Code of 1853 and accepted their lower social status as loyal citizens and accordingly maintained a very low and profile under the Hindu Monarchial system of governance. It may be interesting to note that even after their long presence in Nepal during the monarchy there was hardly any significant communal problem in the kingdom. Living in Hindu scriptures-based cultural milieu and related social environment for centuries they accepted the situation and consequently exclusion and backwardness was institutionalized as a part and parcel of Muslim life in Nepal.

The end of Rana regime in 1951 and establishment of Monarchy-led multi-party coalition government hardly made any change in the social status of the Muslims. The situation more or less remained the same even after 1959 promulgation of constitution and the formation of democratically elected government with B.P. Koirala as Prime Minister. In 1960 King Mahendra dismissed this government and introduced Monarchy-led party less Panchayat system. He replaced the 1853 Old legal Code with a comparatively more modern new Code in 1963, which provided equal citizen status to the Muslims. Although, the new Code allowed the Muslims to practice their religion freely, the ban on conversion or dissolution of marriage etc remained as it was in 1853 Code. Any attempt to convert people religiously remained a punishable offence with three-year imprisonment. It was not possible for Muslims to propagate and do practice religious conversion by Muslims. The King however, nominated one Muslim in his National Panchayati (Parliament) and there was no restriction on opening of *madrassas* (Muslim religious schools).This was the limited freedom provided to Muslim masses of Nepal by Nepali Hindu state. Even though Nepali state provided the Muslim minority with the limited freedom to practice Islam, it also imposed several restrictions. While providing land grants for the construction of mosques and madrassas and establishing cemeteries, for example, it issued a strict ban on proselytizing and cow slaughter. The old Civil Code (*Mulki Ain*) enacted during the rule of Rana Prime Minister Jung Bahadur Rana in 1853 ordered all the communities living within the country into a single hierarchy based on notions of ritual purity and pollution. In the process, the state assigned the Muslims a caste status towards the bottom end of the hierarchy. As with Christians, they were listed among the "impure but not untouchable castes"—in the same category as oil pressers, butchers and washer folk. The new Legal Code (*Mulki Ain*) promulagated in 1963 abolished the caste and religious based discriminations theoretically but in practice caste and religion based discriminations prevails even to these days in the daily lives of Nepali masses.

Historically, the migration of Muslim in Nepal has been a process slow and deliberate, but the states restriction on their rights has been fast and hurried. However, despite various restrictions, the Nepali state failed to restrict the mushrooming growth of Muslim population. Owing to the lack of family control, there has been a gradual increase in Muslim population explained by natural growth arising from a very high fertility rate. The number of conversions to Islam is statistically negligible, and there has been no permanent mass-migration from India. The Muslims of Nepal have never been a part of the landed gentry, as Muslims are elsewhere in South Asia. The average size of Muslim land holdings in Nepal is 0.86 hectares in the Nepali hills and 1.23 hectares in the plains. Many Terai Muslims are engaged as tenants and agriculture wage laborers.

Owing to social and legal handicaps, Muslims have been underrepresented in the system of government in Nepal, and there are few in trade and industry. Nepali Muslims appear to lag behind those of neighboring countries in affluence and political representation but there is a greater feeling of security among them. Terai Muslim has more sense of personal security than those living in India. There have been few outright Hindu-Muslim conflicts in the Nepal Terai. According to the *All Nepal Anjuman Islaha* (ANAI), a Muslim committee appointed by the late King Mahendra to resolve communal problems, there were 12 recorded instances of communal riots in Nepal between 1954 and 1977, a period of 23 years. These riots were mostly provoked by allegations of cow slaughter, religious processions such as the *Tajia*, or the building of mosques. The most serious communal flare up was a 1971 riot in Bara and Rauthat districts, triggered when some Hindus murdered a Muslim on the charge of cow slaughter. These two Terai districts were unstable for two weeks and the situation of the minority Muslims seemed extremely vulnerable. King Mahendra, arriving from a trip abroad, marshaled armed police and suppressed the communal riot. This use of state machinery for their protection seems to have augmented the Nepali Muslims' confidence on the Hindu monarch and state. Owing to this the Muslims of Nepal have a historical mind-set that they are protected because they constitute a small minority and maintain a low profile. The Hindu majority does not feel great animosity towards Islam because Nepal has never faced the trauma of Muslim rule as in the case of India. And then, Nepal has also not undergone the trauma of a partition based on religion as in the case of India. However, long-dormant resentments may exist among some, having to do with Gayasuddin Tuglaq's raid on Simraungad or Samsuddin's pillage of the Kathmandu Valley kingdoms during the 13th century, mass genocide of upper caste Hindus in India during the Muslim rule in India, and the mythical flight of Rajputs and Brahmins from the Indus-Ganga plain to the mid-hills, these are not recent-enough historical experience for them to affect present-day Hindu-Muslim inter-community relations in Nepal.

The demotion of Babri Masjid was an historical event in the context of South Asia. The demolition led to violent communal riots in India, Bangladesh and Pakistan. In Nepal one very interesting incident happened almost immediately after the demolition of Babri Masjid in Ayodhya on 6 December 1992. An idol of Hindu god Krishna was broken by a man in Eastern Nepal. With nerves tattered all around in the fear of communal activity, to everyone's relief he turned out to be not a Muslim but a Hindu frenzied father shocked over the death of his child. While Hindu-Muslim relations have been affected by Ayodhya incident, Nepal did not experience the violence seen by India, Bangladesh and Pakistan. Religiously motivated violent communal incidents have rarely occurred in Nepal. The credit for this largely goes to Nepali politicians who have refrained from playing the religious card. However, the situations are altering after the political changes of 2006 (establishment of Republican democracy) when different ethnic and religious groups are raising the issues of social inclusion and rights consequently the politicians are getting opportunity to play their cards.

Despite the various political changes, the social status of the Muslims did not altered rather it opened a floodgate for the various Ismamist groups from across the boarder to expand their activities in Nepal. With the financial support from Muslim world there was a speedy growth of madrassas and mosques in both sides of 1751 k.m. Indo-Nepal border particularly along the northern Indian states of Uttar Pradesh and Bihar. This has led to a sharp increase in Muslim population of Nepal though the National Census of Nepal 2011 put the Muslim population data in Nepal a little above 4%. However, some Muslim fundamentalist organizations like *Millat-e-Islamia* have alleged that their population comprises 10% of the total population of Nepal. Since the government of Nepal did not approve the hypothetical exaggerated claim of the Muslim organizations, the figure of 10% seems a hoax. However, there is no doubt that Muslim population is increasing in Nepal which is an alarming situation. At the present, four districts of Terai namely Banke, Kapilbastu, Parsa and Rautahat with over fifty percent of Muslim population are now Muslim-majority districts. In five Terai districts namely, Bara, Mahottari, Dhanusha, Sirha and Sunsari Muslims are the second religious majority and in two districts namely Rupandehi and Sarlahi they constitute as a significantly third religious group. Whatever may be the correct figure of Muslims in Nepal, it is something amazing to see how these significant followers of Islam compromised with anti-*Shariat (Islamic laws)* un-Islamic Hindu environment lived here peacefully for centuries. Socio-political scientists might have their own analysis but it gives credence to some views that *Shariat* could be made flexible if it serves the interest of political Islamists.

By and large Muslims of Nepal had a feeling of better security of their life and properties under the Monarchy led party-less Panchayat system in comparison to their counterparts in secular and multi-party democratic India. Muslims in Nepal had a long established apprehension that Hindu-majority parliamentary rule would endanger even their present identity. Such feeling made them complacent and accordingly, their participation in the pro-democracy movement of early 1990 and 2006 was minimal. However, taking advantage of the democratic movement some of the fundamentalist organizations like *Millat-e-Islamia* and *Muslim Seva Samiti* were found expressing concern over the state sponsored drive for Nepalization of the people. The Muslim youths took this move as Hinduization of Muslims.

Political transformation of Nepal from absolute Hindu monarchy to multi-party parliamentary democracy in 1990 was a landmark development in the history of Nepal. The constitution declared Nepal as a multi-ethnic, multi-lingual, democratic, independent, indivisible, sovereign Hindu and constitutional monarchial kingdom. It was said that the state shall not discriminate among citizens on grounds of religion, race, sex, caste, tribe or ideological conviction or any of these. But the reality is different even in 21st century after the second pro-democracy movement and the establishment of democratic republican system of governance. Nevertheless, the sudden rise in political profile of the Muslims not only boosted the morale of this century's old suppressed community but also provided them an opportunity to raise an assertive voice for sharing political and administrative power. Accordingly they raised demands like 10% reservation in constituent assemblies, reserved seats in Parliament and government holidays on Muslim festival. Similarly the radical Islamists also became active to spread their network to struggle for their separate identity with the active support of militant organization of Islamic world.

Although Muslims were not fully satisfied due to Hindu character of the 1990 constitution, they had no problem in their socio-political and religious activities. Some Muslim organizations that were operating as socio-religious organizations became aggressive in challenging their centuries old subordinate status. This led to communal conflicts in some of the districts of Terai region where Muslims are in competitive strength. In Kapilvastu district a violent communal riot erupted in 2005 that ended with the killing of numerous innocent Hindus and Buddhists. The communal riot ended with government interference but the scars of communal violence are still fresh in the minds of Hindu and Buddhist population. The rising strength of Muslim population in Kapilvastu is attributed to cross-border migration of Muslims from Uttar Pradesh and Bihar states of North India. The open border is fueling the Islamic fundamentalists of both sides of the borders.

After the people's revolution of 2006, the Interim Parliament declared Nepal as a secular state on May 18, 2006, and this was endorsed by the interim constitution on May 2007. It says, "Nepal is an independent, invisible, sovereign, secular, inclusive and fully democratic state". Constituent Assembly approved the interim constitution after its election. Nonetheless, the vital question is how far the Muslim masses of Nepal would integrate in the national mainstream and join the nation building programme under a new political environment. However, the answer remains in the womb of future, but if the radical Islamists are not kept under check and political parties imitate the vote-seeking politics, common Muslim masses will remain isolated and backward as they were for centuries. The growth of *madrassas* (Muslim schools) instead of modern schools for modern education and wide network of Islamist terrorists would only add to Muslim misery. Mushrooming growth of Islamic organizations having links with the Radical Islamists of the Islamic world has not only become the concern of the people of Nepal but it is also a security risk for South-Asia and the entire world.

On September 1, 2004, thousands of demonstrators stormed the main mosque in Kathmandu, the capital of Nepal, sets furniture and carpet on fire, tore up a copy of Quran and chanted *Down with Islam*. They were protesting against the killing of twelve innocent Nepalese laborers in Iraq by the Iraqi Islamic terrorists. Police had to open fire to control the crowd. The incident was a signal for the future tension based relation between Hindu and Muslims of Nepal, who were otherwise living peacefully for centuries in the hills and Terai. This is an alarming situation for all. Nevertheless, the Muslims who migrated to Nepal more than five hundred years ago – are as much Nepali as any other groups in Nepal. Muslim culture has also played an important role to integrate Nepalese culture. For centuries, in all ecological zones, Hindus, Buddhists and Muslims lived together respecting each others' religion and culture. The spontaneous religious solidarity shown by different groups just after the communal incident in Kathmandu was an expression of how strong the religious tolerance is in the mind of Nepalese people. Muslim world might have watched all the events that took place in Nepal. From Muslim dominated areas to others, there were a series of programs and rallies organized by different religious group to heal the wound. Nepalese people comprehended the magnitude of religious harmony to sustain Nepal as a multi-religious and multi-ethnic country. Whether Muslim, Buddhist or Hindus, Nepalese are integrated by their inner belief of harmony. At a time when Nepalese society is exposed to the outside world, there is possibility of external influences in certain behavior. The sense of coexistence and religious harmony integrates Nepalese society but caustic elements intend to disrupt this centuries old co-existence. Despite religious and other differences, from hills to Terai and capital, Hindu, Muslims and other religious groups are integrated with each other. Muslims of the hills speak fluent local language and Muslims in hill live amicably with Hindus and other ethnic groups there. The Muslim religion also plays important role to integrate traditional Nepalese culture. Unlike other countries in south Asia, Muslims are mixed up and are the part of Nepalese society. Without the supply of bangles and beads (called *Chura, Pote* in Nepali) and other ornaments by hill Muslims (*Churoute*) who make them, marriage of Hindu people cannot be complete in the hills. Without the contribution of Muslims, Hindu's culture is incomplete. A married Hindu woman needs a long straight bar of jewelry (glass beads) and bangles (called *Chura* in Nepali) made by Muslims.

Nepal has been a melting pot of diverse cultural groups, where today a systematic cultural assimilation is taking place and Muslims, Buddhists and Hindus and other religious groups all have their own share in Nepalese culture. However, for the Muslims as religious alien it has been a great challenge to assimilate them culturally, religiously, economically and politically in the mainstream Nepalese society. Nepal has been a prolific ground for different groups from both South (India) and North (China). It has been a safe haven where different ethnic and religious groups fused and melted. Muslims migrated to Nepal as traders. Even during the period of national unification by Shah Dynasty King Prithvi Narayan Shah some 245 years ago, he had invited some Muslims to do various tasks in Nepal. Gurkhas used the weapons like guns developed by Muslims to fight against the British imperial rulers of India during the Anglo-Nepalese war of 1814. Hence Muslims have played a vital role in national unification of Nepal. The legalistic path of the *Sufism* and *sharia* had a profound impact on the growth of Islam in south Asia. A Sufi attains a direct vision of oneness with God, often on the edges of orthodox behavior, and can thus become a *Pir* (living saint) who may take on disciples (*murids*) and set up a spiritual lineage that can last for generations. Orders of Sufis became important in India during the thirteenth century following the path of Moinuddin Chishti (1142–1236), who settled in Ajmer, Rajasthan, and attracted large numbers of converts to Islam because of his holiness. His *Chishtiyya* order went on to become the most influential Sufi lineage in India, although other orders from Central Asia and Southwest Asia also reached India and played a major role in the spread of Islam in Nepal Terai and in hills (Miller, 2009). In this way, they created a large literature in regional languages that embedded Islamic culture deeply into older South Asian traditions. Nevetheless, conflicts and strife between Hindus and Muslims has got a historical legacy and has became a common phenomenon in South Asia specially India. The reason for "Hindu - Muslim" conflict is "Hindu Backlash" or "partial" secularism, in which only Hindus are expected to be secular while Muslims and other minorities remain free to practice exclusionary practices (Sikand, 2004). Muslims with quite different religious traditions and etiquettes amid the stigma of a religious alien, their social-economic, religious and political status remained dismal. Likewise, probable threat of the rise of Islamic religious fundamentalism in the remote hills and Terai of Nepal may be an issue of serious concern not only for the Nepalese rulers but for all conscious governments of the region including India.

Muslims of Nepal have desire that Nepal's Muslim community should be recognized as a distinct entity. Muslim leaders used to reiterate government and parties that Muslims are not just a "vote bank", and they demand specific steps in favor of Muslims. The Muslim's of Nepal wants the country's government to acknowledge that Nepali Muslims have a separate identity, and that demands the creation of a separate Islamic Affairs Commission, an Islamic School (*Madrassah*) Board, a *Hajj* Committee (for annual pilgrimages to Mecca) and the introduction of Islamic personal law based on *Sharia* for Muslims. Nepali Muslims think they should not be exploited as a mere scapegoat. But, neither the government, nor political parties have paid attention to Muslim concerns; no effort has been made to launch any concrete programmes targeting the Muslim community.

Muslims, amid the raising population, constitute Nepal's second largest religious minority after Buddhists. At the present, the Nepalese Muslims are asking for special provisions for Muslims in the new constitution to be drafted by the constitution assembly. They are also asking for amendments in the interim republican constitution which makes special provisions and privileges for disadvantaged groups like women, low caste Dalits, and ethnic communities but does not mention Muslims. The government's decision to reserve seats for backward communities in the now secular republic has stirred up a hornets' nest. The Muslims, along with ethnic groups from the Terai plains, fear that the reservation policy will favour only the Madhesis (people of Terai region) and the people of Indian origin living in the Terai. They are now demanding an amendment in the constitution so that Muslims are included as a separate group among disadvantaged communities. Like other protesting groups, Nepal's Muslims too want proportional representation in all state organs on the basis of population. Muslims are demanding a new census in order to be better represented. The Nepalese government has signed an agreement with representatives of the Muslim community granting them political, social and cultural rights as a way to stave off possible separatist tendencies. The agreement however ignores the inclusion in the constitution of *Sharia*-based personal law as demanded by the Nepalese Muslim. In the perspective of hill Muslims, the situation is grim owing to their unfavorable geographical locations. Living in lofty hill surrounded by majority Hindus has created crisis in security situation. Dominance of Hindu doctrines in day to day life, discriminations of various sorts in practice----social, cultural, religious, political etc, inadequate legal protection and isolation from their fellow brothers inhabiting in plain Terai regions has further exacerbated the problems of hill Muslims (*Churoute)* who are making their livelihood in remote parts of Nepal amid religious discriminations, backwardness and poverty.

The paucity or poor exists where people fall short of reasonably defined minimum levels of wellbeing such as access to certain consumption or income levels , housing, health and education facilities and certain rights recognized according to standards of human needs and socio economic conditions of the society. Therefore a poverty line may be defined as the minimum level required acquiring by the poor to escape the poverty thereby identifying poor. The poverty gap is defined as the requirement of money (shortfall) by a poor to come out of the poverty or gap between the total consumption value of a poor and the value of the poverty line. The Poverty Gap Index (PGI or P1) is a standard measure of the depth of the poverty that averages the ratios of shortfalls to the value of poverty line over both poor and non-poor assuming zero shortfalls for non -poor and presents as a percentage. The measure of shortfall quantifies the poverty gap in terms of money required to escape the poverty hence provide more information than headcount to poverty alleviation policy makers and assistance to precise allocation of resources. Presence of high inequality in possession of resources and access to basic consumption needs among people or social segments is attributed to an unjust society that leads to several social conflicts. The Poverty Gap Index is the measure for severity of poverty by means of the inequality among poor. Closely embedded with *poverty or plenty* issue is development issue. However, the sweet slogan of development has too often failed to deliver on its promises to poor. The policies imposed from above by international agencies and state bodies have frequently not met the needs and aspirations of ordinary people. Development agencies have been searching for sometime for alternative approaches. One of those being pioneered is *indigenous knowledge* which aims to make local voices heard more effectively. However, while it is increasingly acknowledged in development contexts, it is yet to be validated and accepted by social scientists especially anthropologists. It is self-evident to any anthropologist that effective development assistance will benefit from some understanding of local knowledge and practices. This therefore puts anthropology and anthropologists at the centre of development. There are two major issues that anthropology might profitably address. First of all how to define indigenous knowledge and who should define it as it currently lacks disciplinary coherence. Secondly once this definition is achieved what methodologies should be used in such an interdisciplinary research endeavor when it must meet the demands of development (cost- and time-effective, intelligible to non-experts) while not compromising anthropological expectations **(Bicker, Pottier, Sillitoe, 2004).**

Closely allied to development issues is class concept. Classes often have a distinct lifestyle that emphasizes their class The most powerful class in a society often uses markers such as costume, grooming, manners and language codes that mark insiders and outsiders; unique political rights such as honorary titles; and, concepts of social honour or face that are claimed to only be applicable to the in group. But each class has distinctive features, often becoming defining elements of personal identity and uniting factors in group behaviour. There prevails a notion of high and low classes with a distinction between bourgeois tastes and sensitivities and the working class tastes and sensitivities (Bourdieu, and Wacquan, 1992).

Marxism's central premise is that human nature is characterized by the capacity for creative and purposive action- "labor"- that has effects in the establishment of material culture. When agriculture enabled human being to produce a surplus of food conflicts arose in society over these products and over control of the labor process initiating a process of social differentiating and growing inequality (Encyclopedia of Sociology, 2003). Karl Marx saw humans as being unique by virtue of their conscious awareness of themselves and their situation, According to Marx they are capable of self – reflection and hence, assessment of their positions in society. Such consciousness arises out of people's daily existence and is not a realm of ideas that is somehow independent of the material world, as much German philosophy argued. For Marx, people produce their ideas conceptions of the world in the light of the social structures in which they are born, raised and live. The world around is a materialization of man's praxis; his productive activity in history is not just an assertion that nature is man made. It also means that man's understanding of the material world is a reflection of his own social world. Marx claimed that the history of all hitherto existing society is the history of class struggle. He says *free man and* *slave, patrician and plebian, lord and serf, guild master and Journey man in a word, oppressor and oppressed, stood in constant apposition to one another, carried on an uninterrupted, now hidden, now open fight that each time ended either in a revolutionary reconstruction of society at large or in the common ruin of contending classes.* In the modern Nepalese history diverse sorts of conflicts occurred due to hegemony of dominant group on subordinates, backwardness, ignorance, suppression and exploitation. Marxist perspective developed by Karl Marx with his thought and belief on proletariat relate to Muslim peoples life and their social-economic status, tribulation and implications.

The Marxist conception of class involves a collective group of individuals that share similar economic and social relations relative to each other in society. A class is a group with intrinsic tendencies and interests that are different from, and may be opposed to the interests of other groups in society. For example, it is in the laborers best interest to maximize wages and benefits and in the elite's best interest to maximize profit at the expense of such, leading to a contradiction within the system, even if the laborers and elites themselves are unaware of these class dichotomies. There are two factors involved with class:

Objective factors

A class shares a common relationship to the means of production. That is, all people in one class make their living in a common way in terms of ownership of the things that produce social goods. A class may own things, own land, own people, be owned, but some own nothing but their labor. A class will extract tax, produce agriculture, enslave and make others work, be enslaved and work, or work for a wage.

Subjective factors

The members will necessarily have some perception of their similarity and common interest and this is class consciousness. Class consciousness is not simply an awareness of one's own class interest (for instance, the maximization of shareholder value; or, the maximization of the wage with the minimization of the working day); class consciousness also embodies deeply shared views of how society should be organized legally, culturally, socially and politically. The first criteria divide a society into the owners and non-owners of means of production. In capitalism, these are capitalist (bourgeoisie) and proletariat. Finer divisions can be made, however: the most important subgroup in capitalism being petite bourgeoisie (small bourgeoisie), people who possess their own means of production but utilize it primarily by working on it themselves rather than hiring others to work on it. They include people working as laborers abroad, self-employed artisans, small shopkeepers, and many low ranking professionals as in the case of Muslims of Nepal. A prerequisite for classes is existence of sufficient surplus product. Marxists explain the history of civilized societies in terms of a war of classes between those who control production and those who produce the goods or services in society. In the Marxist view of capitalism, this is a conflict between capitalists (bourgeoisie) and wage-workers (the proletariat). For Marxists, class antagonism is rooted in the situation that control over social production necessarily entails control over the class which produces goods—in capitalism this is the exploitation of workers by the bourgeoisie.

Marx squabble that it was the goal of the proletariat itself to displace the capitalist system with socialism, changing the social relationships underpinning the class system and then developing into a future communist society in which: .. *The free development of each is the condition for the free development of all.* This would mark the beginning of a classless society in which human needs rather than profit would be motive for production. In a society with democratic control and production for use, there would be no class, no state and no need for money. Russian communist leader Vladimir Lenin defined classes as large groups of people differing from each other by the place they occupy in a historically determined system of social production, by their relation (in most cases fixed and formulated in law) to the means of production, by their role in the social organization of labor, and, consequently, by the dimensions of the share of social wealth of which they dispose and the mode of acquiring it.

The most important transformation of society for Marxists has been the enormous and speedy growth of the proletariats in the world population during the last two hundred and fifty years. Starting with agricultural and domestic textile laborers in England and Flanders, more and more occupations only provide a living through wages or salaries Private enterprise or self-employment in a variety of occupations is no longer as viable as it once was, and so many people who once controlled their own labor-time are converted into proletarians. Today groups which in the past subsisted on stipends or private wealth—like academics, doctors or lawyers—are now increasingly working as wage laborers Marxists call this process proletariatisation, and point to it as the major factor in the proletariat being the largest class in current societies. The increasing dissolution of the peasant-lord relationship (pre-capitalist societies), initially in the commercially active and industrializing countries, and then in the unindustrialized countries as well, has virtually eliminated the class of peasants. Poor rural laborers still exist, but their current relationship with production is predominantly as landless wage labourers or rural proletarians. The destruction of the peasantry, and its conversion into a rural proletariat, is largely a result of the general proletariatisation of all work. This process is today largely complete, although it was arguably incomplete in the 1960s and 1970s. Nevertheless, a vast majority of the world's people are living in acute poverty, and lack access to many basic resources, services and rights. They face problems and challenges that are difficult for the citizens of the developed countries to understand. It is even harder for the governments to find ways of helping these people solve their economic, social and political problems. **Underdevelopment** is a term often used to refer to **economic underdevelopment**, symptoms of which include backwardness, lack of access to job opportunities, health care, drinkable water, food, education and housing.

Underdevelopment as in the case of least developed Nepal takes place when resources are not used to their full social-economic potential, with the result that local or regional development is slower in most cases than it should be. Furthermore, it results from the complex interplay of internal and external factors that allow less developed communities only a lop-sided development progression. Underdeveloped nations as Nepal are characterized by a wide disparity between their rich and poor populations living in rural and urban areas.

Class struggle constitutes the central theme of Marx's theoretical scheme, which is based on the premises that *the history of all hitherto existing society is the history of class struggles.* Freeman and slave, patrician and plebian, lord and serf, guild master and journeyman, in a word, oppressor and oppressed, stood in constant opposition to one another, carried on an uninterrupted, now hidden, now open fight, a fight that each time enter in a revolutionary reconstitution of society at large or in the common ruin of the contending classes. In the context of Muslims of Nepal, they have been debarred from getting an entry in ruling class groups of the dominant

Hindu mainstream owing to which they are dominated, exploited and have been suppressed and treated as second class citizen in the rural and urban societies.

In the capitalist society, the bourgeoisie and proletariat are two different classes and are dependent upon each other. However, the mutual dependency of the two classes is not a relationship of equability and of respectable reciprocity. Instead, it is a relationship of exploiter, exploited, oppressor, and oppressed. The capitalist class (the ruling class) gains at the expense of the labor class (the subject class) and there is therefore a conflict of interest between them. Marx developed his theory of class conflict in his analysis and critique of the capitalist society (Rao, 2002). In Miyagaon, Hukka the class of poor Muslims and the urban dwellers elite varies and diverges on assorted issues related to rights to land, land ownership, property etc. Hence, it is clear that the notion of class conflict has provided enticement for the study of Muslims of Nepal.

From the Marxist perspective, in all stratified societies there are two major social groups; a rich class and poor class, or the 'Have and Have-Not'; or a ruling class and subject class. The key to understanding a given society is to discover which the dominant mode of production within it is. From a Marxian view, a class is a social group where members share the same relationships to the forces of production. Thus, during the feudal stage, there are two main classes distinguished by their relationship to land, the major force of production. Marxist perspective holds the notion that more the unequal is the distribution of scarce resources in a system; the greater is the conflict of interest between dominant and subordinate segments in a system. The inferior segments become sentient of their true collective interests, the more probable are they to inquire the legitimacy of the existing pattern of distribution of scarce resources. The more social changes brought by governing segments interrupt existing relations among subordinates; the more likely are the latter to become aware of their true interest. The more the performances of leading segments create alienative temperament among subsidiaries; the more likely are the latter to become responsive of their true collective interest. If the dominants are more polarized, the more violent is their conflict. If the conflict is more violent, greater structural changes will occur the scarce resources will be distributed in a fair way. Thus, Marxist anthropology defines society in terms of conflict and change (Turner, 1998). Pedestal to this logic, I propose that owing to the unfair hegemony of dominant group on subordinates, unequal distribution of resources in feudal Nepalese society, especially the mainstreams privileged upper caste Hindus and the *religious alien* Muslims, a violent conflict or collision of some sort may crop up in future.

The role of education in the context of social exclusion, development and backwardness has been guided by several questions. One of the major question asked is, how is the educational system shaped by the economic infrastructure? Louis Althusser, Samuel Bowles Herbert Gintis and Ivan Illich (2004) have provided a general framework and supported the Marxian perspective. Although in sympathy with much of what Illich says, Marxists such as Bowles and Gintis argue that he has made a fundamental error. Rather than seeing schools as the basis of problem and their removal as its solution, Bowles and Gintis argue that, 'The social problem to which these reforms are addressed have their roots not primarily in the school system itself, but rather in the normal functioning of the economic system'. From their viewpoint, de-schooling would only produce 'occupational misfits' and 'job blues' which are hardly sufficient to transform society as a whole. Not only this, school students will be a direct victim of social exclusion prevalent in various forms – social, cultural, economic, educational, religious, etc. Primarily, through language and culture, the ruling elites excluded all others from the mainstream of development for centuries. This is what has been customarily continuing in South Asian Countries – mainly in Nepal. In a broad spectrum, social exclusion is a process by which certain groups are systematically disadvantaged because they are discriminated against on the basis of their religion, ethnicity, race, sexual orientation, caste, descent, gender, age, disability, HIV status, migrant status or where they live. Discrimination occurs in public institutions such as the legal system or education and health services as well as social institutions like the household and in the community (Beall & Piron, 2005). While there is a considerable debate about the precise meaning of the term, some of the most useful definitions have sought to emphasize that social exclusion is concerned with the inability to participate effectively in economic, social, and cultural life and, in some characteristics, alienation and distance from mainstream society (Duffy, 1995). From Marxian perspective, liberation involves a revolutionary change and this perspective prepares a ground for evaluating the education related social status of the Muslims of Kihun.

Embedded with social exclusion, people's livelihood and social-economic issues is the topic of poverty. Poverty is a condition wherein a person cannot satisfy his or her basic needs, namely, food, shelter, clothing, health and education. Poverty is pronounced deprivation in well-being, and comprises many dimensions. It includes low incomes and the inability to acquire the basic goods and services necessary for survival with dignity. **Embedded with social-economic status *poverty* is the precarious issue. It** is the deficiency of basic human needs such as clean water, nutrition, health care, education, clothing and shelter, because of the powerlessness to manage to pay for them. This is also referred to as *absolute poverty* or **destitution.** On the other hand *relative poverty* is the condition of having fewer resources or less income than others within a society or country, or compared to worldwide averages. Historically poverty reduction has been a result of economic growth as increased levels of production, such as modern industrial technology, made more wealth available for those who were otherwise too poor to afford them. Poverty encompasses low levels of health and education, poor access to clean water and sanitation, inadequate physical security, lack of voice, and insufficient capacity and opportunity to better one's life. Fundamentally, poverty is a denial of choices and opportunities, a violation of human dignity. It means lack of basic capacity to participate effectively in society. It means not having enough to feed and cloth of family, not having a school or clinic to go to, not having the land on which to grow one's food or a job to earn one's living, and not having access to credit. It means insecurity, powerlessness and exclusion of individuals, households and communities, susceptibility to violence, and it often implies living in marginal or dangerous environments, without access to clean water or sanitation. The reasons behind poverty are manifold. Education and healthcare does not reach the common people. Due to lack of jobs, people are forced to migrate to large cities for temporary work. For those unable to find jobs the result is poverty. Poor health and education severely affects productivity at work. Inadequate nutrition in childhood undermines the ability of individuals to develop their full physical mental capabilities. Lack of essential minerals such as iodine and iron can harm brain development. Resolution to poverty is economic growth and development. Although economic growth and development are similar in meaning, they have some essential differences. Economic growth refers to the increasing ability to produce more goods and services. Economic development implies that individuals will be better off and takes into account changes in economic and social structures that will reduce or eliminate poverty. Economic development can be measured in a number of different ways including the Human Development Index, a Gender Empowerment Measure, a Human Poverty Index and a Human Freedom Index. Economic growth is the expansion of a country's productive capacity (**Cainen**, 2007). This leads to a rise in total national output. Growth can occur in two different ways; the increased use of land, labor, capital and commercial resources by using better technology or management techniques and increased productivity of existing resource use through rising labor and capital productivity. While theoretically having an increasing national output means greater material welfare and a rise in living standards, it does not equate to having higher levels of well being for individuals in that nation. Economic growth can, in fact, have negative impacts on a nation including environmental degradation and the loss of traditional cultural values. It also may mean there is greater inequality between different classes in society, that is, the gap between the rich and the poor may grow as is in the case of the current study on Muslim.

Anthropologists and sociologists persist to see economy and society as intertwined, but sociologists came to accept the emerging division between the disciplines. Sociologists were inductive, deriving theories of social behavior by observing behavior. Economists were deductive, deriving theories of economic behavior from the axiom that self-interest drives individual behavior. Sociology became increasingly empirical, based on in-depth studies of communities and corporations and sectors of the economy. C. Wright Mills's *The Power Elite* (1956) showed that power was becoming increasingly concentrated in business, government, and the military and that links between the elites in those sectors were increasing. Sociologists began to explain economic behavior in terms of four social mechanisms they had observed shaping all sorts of social behavior. These mechanisms entered the common lexicon under the terms *institution*, *network*, *power*, and *cognition*.

Sociology's core insight is that individuals behave according to scripts that are tied to social roles. Those scripts are called conventions at the collective level and cognitive schemas at the individual level. Conventions and schemas make sense within a wider institutional framework, be it rational or religious or mystical. These conventions and schemas shape individual behavior and so predicting economic behavior is a matter of comprehending conventions, schemas, and institutions. But prediction requires more than that, because conventions change. Understanding why they change is job one and change can usually be traced to institutions, power, networks, and cognition. Economic *institutions* offer broad prescriptions for behavior. Institutions are sustained by occupational, industrial, and community *networks* that define social roles. *Power* shapes the evolution of new customs, when the powerful sanction the behavior of others and when they shape legal institutions. At the individual level, *cognition* is the carrier of conventions--it provides the schemas through which we make ongoing sense of conventions and through which we challenge them (Dobbin, 2004).

Economic sociologists take a diverse view of why economic institutions vary across nations, why particular institutions persist, and what causes institutions to change. On the issue of why different kinds of economic systems arose in the first place, institutional analysts from political science and sociology argue that history has given different societies different material to begin with. On the issue of why economic institutions change, Weber argued that change could originate in politics, in the law and in religious ideals. Customs tend to persist until something shakes up the social system, opening up the possibility of change. New customs are often worked out in power struggles, and they may or may not be more efficient than those they replace. This concept of new customs worked out in power struggle provides new enticement for study on Muslims of Nepal as the prevailing customs are on the verge of change owing to the changing trends of the society.

3

GLIMPSES OF THE REGION AND THE MUSLIMS

This study site is the Miyagaon, Hukka region of Kihun VDC of Tanahun district of western Nepal where hills Muslims (*Churoute*) are living for centuries in the rural fringe. The total population of Tanahun district is 323,288 with a male population of 143,410 and a female population of 179,878. The total households number in this district stands at 78309 (Central Bureau of Statistics (CBS), 2011). In this district, the total number of hill Muslims households is 512 with a total population of 3227 members. In the Miyagaon, Hukka area of Kihun Village Development Committee (VDC), there are altogether 64 households of hill Muslims with a total population of 466 members. This book makes a perusal of 64 households of Muslims of Miyagaon, Hukka of Kihun Village. This ethnic religious minority of this region has been selected because:

a) *This region has the highest numbers of hill Muslims in a fixed settlement in the whole western region of Nepal and socially, economically, politically and religiously they are the most vulnerable group and has been affected by the vicious cycle of exclusion and there prevail among them trends of poverty vs. plenty and traditional vs. modern dichotomies.*

b) They also represent diverse characteristics (social-economic, cultural etc) as they are living in close contact with other groups for centuries with high influence of Hinduization and Sanskritization processes.

Brief Introduction of Tanahun District

Tanahun District, a part of Gandaki Zone, is one of the seventy five districts of Nepal. It has historical identity as a powerful state among Parbat, Tanahun and Kaski, the petty independent states before 1840. Most of the parts are the watershed area of the rivers like Marshyangdi, Trisuli, Kali, Madi, Seti etc. At first the founder of Nepali nation Prithvi Narayan Shah had failed to unify Tanahun in his mission in 1770 during his campaign of building a greater Nepal. Later, Tanahun was annexed by his successors in 1840.

Nevertheless, before unification Tanahun had extensive area which was extended to Chitwan district of central Nepal, Bihar of India, the western part of Champaran (Bihar), which includes Ramnagar and Betia. It was merged and annexed into the greater Nepal at the time of Pratap Singh Shah and Rajendra Laxmi the successors of king Prithvi Narayan Shah. The district, with Damauli as its district headquarters, covers an area of 1,546 km^2 (CBS, 2011).The district headquarters Damauli is located in the centre of *Vyas* municipality, which was declared as municipality by Nepalese government in 1991. It is the historical place of *Panchayan* temple, *Vyas* cave, the adjacent area of Madi and Seti River, saint *Parasar* cave etc. The name of Vyas municipality is derived from the mythological Hindu saint (*Rishi* in Sanskrit) of Mahabharata era *Vyas*. It is called the birth place and yoga place of Rishi Vyas, the great Hindu scholar saint.

Prithwi Highway crossed through east to west in this district. Bandipur was the headquarters of Tanahun district till 1968. The business activities were at its peak, especially for the transitional purpose between Tibet and India. The construction of Prithvi highway supported the transportation and business activities. Damauli, Dumre, Khaireni, Dule Gauda, Bhimbad are the vital areas of Tanahun district.

There are different views about the naming of Tanahun district. There are three hilly peaks at the Tanahun district's historical headquarters Tanahunsur; they are called "*Tritung*", which is the base for naming Tanahun, the first evidence. Second, there are various places in which the last alphabet is made by prefix *hun* like Kihun, Kahung, Manhun etc so that it was named *Tanahun*. From administrative point of view Nepal is divided into 14 zones and 75 districts with special diversities. Tanahun district is a mosaic of diverse cultures of different ethnicities. It is rich in indigenous ethnic cultures, customs, traditions, life pattern and ethnic diversities. It may be a laboratory for social researchers. The physiographic condition of Tanahun is made of different land features like high hills and valley plains. Valleys and plain land were no men's land before the eradication of malaria in the mid 20th century. However, the hills were crowded by human settlements.

Geography, economic, political conditions, demographical, social and cultural aspects create impacts on natural resource management and development practices of a region. Tanahun district is an example. Despite abundance of natural resources, the district is backward. Various characteristics and features are found in this district nevertheless the district is far from the race of development. It is a verity that despite the ambitious local governance act in 1990s in Nepal, relationship between centers, sub-centers and peripheries remained strongly hierarchical in terms of institutional structure, information exchange and program and service delivery. High profile government machinery and all the development infrastructures are centralized in the district headquarters or in National capital Kathmandu. The flow of information, decisions and resources remained largely controlled by the central administration in Kathmandu or sub-central authorities in district headquarters of Tanahun district at Damauli.

From physiographic point of view Tanahun district is divided into three main divisions which are as follows:

(1) The hill area of cold-temperate climatic region

Tanahun district is mainly a hilly district with some plain regions also. In broad-spectrum the area is located above 1220 meter from sea level. These are the area of semi-tropical climatic region crowded with human settlements.

(2) Low land

Low land called *Tars* in Nepali are located at the height of 1220 meter. The district is renowned for low land. Some are found the coastal area of rivulets. These areas belong to semi-tropical climatic regions. The main plain lands (called *Phats* in Nepali) and *Tars* of Tanahun are Naudi Phat, Khalte, Kalimati, Baisjangar, Purkot, Dordor, Chundi, Badahare, Turture, Phaundi, Chambas, Bahrabise, Dumre, Satrasaya, Yampa, Nahala, Maibal, Majhuwa, Sange, Damauli, Buldi, Gunadi, Tharpu, Bhimbad,

Dumrebasi, Puttar, Gopha, Keladi, Baindi, Risti, Chhabdi, Kalasti, Naranga, Sukhaura etc.

(3) Inner Pradesh

The areas of Kali Gandaki and Narayani region are Called Inner Pradesh. These areas are located at the height of 735 feet above sea level. Basically the religious places Dev Ghat, Gohitar are the areas of sub-tropical climatic regions. Due to different topographical variations the whole district includes diverse regions.

Historically, Tanahun district is important for mineral resources. In the past, iron ore was found in Dhor area, which was used for the construction of bridge e.g. the Bridge of Seti River in Bhimad area. Likewise, slate chalk, copper was also found in different parts of Tanahun districts in the past but at the present there has been no scientific extraction of ores and minerals. From religious point of view, Dhor Baraha, Chhabdi Baraha, Dev Ghat is the famous religious shrines. Thousands of Hindu pilgrims make a pilgrimage to these places. There are some historical *kots* (forts situated at the top of the hill area basically famous for military and religious purposes). The forts were important from strategic military point of view in the past. But now these forts are abandoned ruins.

Social-economic Profile

From international perspective, Nepal's importance is not only in its size and natural resources but because of its strategic location between two powerful countries China and India. China and India as regional superpowers has been in severe competition since the mid fifties to be the hegemonic leaders in influencing and leading the Asian countries. Because of this rivalry these two countries were involved in border battle in 1962. India regards China as a national threat and hence the strategic importance of Nepal increases as it lies as a buffer zone between India and China. India takes Nepal as an extension of its northern boundary. India's concerns for its security have been acknowledged by United States and Russia. Due to the geopolitical location and strategic importance of Nepal, India is increasing its presence in Nepal through economic, diplomatic and other assistances to prevent Chinese influence in Nepal. Before the emergence of the modern concept of citizenship, Prithvi Narayan Shah the founder of modern Nepal in the eighteenth century, in the name of nationalism, had favored giving citizenship rights to his citizens especially the hill dwellers, exceptional to Indians under certain conditions. However, the modern Nepali nationalism, largely conceived and institutionalized in the latter half of the twentieth century, was shaped around the monarchy, Hinduism and the Nepali language. These restrictive concepts have always excluded plain region, Terai people and religious minorities Muslims, whose distinct cultures and cross-border links have led hill Nepalese to view them with suspicion and derision. The psychological distance between Terai people and the Nepali state, as well as other minorities, was motivated by discriminatory hill dominated Hindu policies. Some of this distance is centuries old but much reflects the more deliberate constructs of autocratic Rana and partyless Panchayat policies. The Panchayat slogan "*ek desh, ek bhesh, ek bhasa*" (one country, one dress, one language) during 1961-1990, proved perilous to minority groups. The cumulative effect as a form of *internal colonization* proved to be precarious and demanded emancipation from dominance of all sorts-social-cultural and political by the ethnic and religious minorities in a predominantly Hindu dominated Nepali state. The prevailing social and economic realties prepared a fertile ground for this.

Social-economic dimensions are closely embedded with social classes. Social classes are the hierarchical arrangements of people in society as economic or cultural groups. Class is an essential object of analysis for sociologists, anthropologists, political economists, and social historians. In social sciences, social class is often discussed in terms of 'social stratification'. In sociology and political philosophy, the most basic class distinction is between the powerful and the powerless. In Marxist theory and historical materialism, social class is caused by the fundamental economic structure of work and property. Various social and political theories propose that social classes with greater power attempt to cement their own ranking above the lower social classes in the social hierarchy to the detriment of the society overall. By contrast, conservatives and structural functionalists have presented class difference as intrinsic to the structure of any society and to that extent ineradicable. Social classes with a great deal of power are usually viewed as "the elites" within their own societies (Barnard et. al., 2004).

Classes often have a distinct lifestyle that emphasizes their class The most powerful class in a society often uses markers such as costume, grooming, manners and language codes that mark insiders and outsiders;

unique political rights such as honorary titles; and, concepts of social honour or face that are claimed to only be applicable to the in group. But each class has distinctive features, often becoming defining elements of personal identity and uniting factors in group behaviour. French sociologist Pierre Bourdieu suggests a notion of high and low classes with a distinction between bourgeois tastes and sensitivities and the working class tastes and sensitivities. Race and other large-scale groupings can also influence class standing. The association of particular ethnic groups with class statuses is common in many societies. As a result of conquest or internal ethnic and religious differentiation, a ruling class is often ethnically and religiously homogenous (such as high caste Hindus in Nepal) and particular races, ethnic or religious groups in some societies such as Muslim community of Nepal, are legally or customarily restricted to occupying particular class positions. Which ethnicities and religious groups are considered as belonging to high or low classes varies from society to society.

Different consumption of social goods is the most visible consequence of class. In modern societies, it manifests as income inequality, though in subsistence Nepali society it is manifested as malnutrition and failure to meet basic needs due to acute poverty. Although class status is not a causal factor for income, in Tanahun district, higher classes have higher incomes than lower classes. This inequality persists when controlling for occupation. The conditions at work vary greatly depending on class. In this district, those in the upper-middle class and middle-class enjoy greater freedoms in their occupations. They generally are more respected, enjoy more diversity, and are able to exhibit some authority. Those in lower classes tend to feel more alienated and have lower work satisfaction overall. The economic conditions of the people in Tanahun district differ greatly between classes. Class has direct consequences on people's lifestyle. Lifestyle includes tastes, preferences, and a general style of living. These lifestyles could quite possibly affect educational attainment, and status attainment. Class lifestyle also affects how children are raised and what sorts of cultural norms are taught.

Demographical Structure

The population trend of Tanahun district is diverse. According to population census of Nepal 2011, the population of Tanahun district is 323,288. Total households number is 78,309. The female population is 179,878 and male population is 143,410.The number of females is quite high. The literacy rate of Tanahun district is 73%. The demographic data of Tanahun district is given in table.

Table 3. 1

The Demographic Structure of Tanahun District

S.N.	Particulars	Census 2011
1.	Total Population	323,288
2.	Male	143,410
3.	Female	179,878
4.	Total Households	78,309
5.	Literacy Rate %	73%

Source: Population Monograph of Nepal, Central Bureau of Statistics, 2011

Different prominent caste/ethnic communities such as Hindu Brahmins and Chettries, Thakuri, Kami, Damai, Sarki, Sanyasi, ethnic groups Magar, Gurung, Newar, Gharti, Kumal, Darai, Tamang, religious minority Muslim and many other marginal groups dwell here. Magar ethnic group is in great majority. Hindu Brahmins are in second position. Caste and ethnic diversity is found in this region. In broad spectrum, in Tanahun district there are 15 ethnic groups registered in *Nepal Aadibasi Janajati Mahasang* (Nepal Ethnic and Indigenous Nationalities). There are multiple ethnic groups which are not identified or registered. Minority ethnic groups registered in Adibasi/Janajati as ethnic groups are Bote, Dura, Thakali, Chepang, Kusunda, Rai, Limbu, Baramu and Bhujel. Such indigenous nationalities comprise more than 50% percent of total population of this district. Hindu Brahmin, Chhetri and Thakuri groups covers approximate 29 percent and low caste occupational Hindu Dalits such as Kami (Blacksmith), Damai (Tailor) and Sarki (Cobbler) comprise above 14 percent and the rests belong to other castes/ethnicities.

The categorization of indigenous ethnic groups is revealed in table 3.2.

Table 3.2

Categorization of Indigenous Ethnic Groups in Tanahun District

S.N.	Class	Ethnic/Caste
1.	Endangered Group	Kusunda

2.	High Marginalized Group	Chepang, Bote and Baramu
3.	Marginalized Group	Tamang, Bhujel, Kumal, Dura and Darai
4.	Disadvantaged Group	Magar, Gurung, Marphali Thakali, Rai, Limbu
5.	Advantaged Group	Newar and Thakali

Source: District Development Committee, Tanahun district, 2011

Population by Religion

People belonging to various religions live in Tanahun district and there seems to be a good religious tolerance among the people. There are various temples, mosques, monasteries, churches in this district. People used to visit and honor all religions. So far there has been no conflict in the name of religion in this district. Majority people have belief in Hinduism that has shaped their attitude, nature and behavior. Buddhism has second position and Islam occupy third position respectively. Christianity, Jain and Sikh are in minority. Tanahun is the district highly influenced by Sanskritization. Hindu epic *Ramayana* has played a major role for Sanskritization and Hinduization of various tribal ethnic groups. One and a half centuries back, the Sanskrit poet Bhanubhakta Acharya of Chudi Ramgha village of this district had translated the Sanskrit *Ramayana* into simple Nepali. His *Ramayana* has created a deep impact on Nepali folk life. The population of this district by religion is monotonous with a Hindu population of more than 83%.

Table 3.3

Population of Tanahun by Religions

Religious groups	Number	Percentage
Hindu	262,164	83.16
Buddhism	47313	14.01
Islam	3227	1.01
Other religions	10584	1.82

Source: Population Monograph of Nepal, Central Bureau of Statistics, 2011

Education

Education enhances the human capacity. It is linked with economy and livelihood of the common people. It opens the way to survive in modern age by enabling people to face the present challenges of livelihood. Education accumulates human knowledge and discharges it when needed. It helps the social change. Education selects and categories the difference between human and animal. The purpose of education may be to instill discipline and respect or to give everyone an equal chance to broaden their intellectual and emotional life. Some people would say it provides a small minority with an intensive, high equality process of intellectual stimulation until they are adult, and gives the poorer majority a lower quality basic education until they are in their adolescence. Others believe education operates to reproduce the capitalist class system, gender roles and patriarchal relationship (Barnard et.al, 2004).

Although education in the Nepalese context may be playing prime role in strengthening patriarchal relationship, there subsist no qualm that education is an important attribute for the development of human personality and leadership skill so that to work in any kind of development or management works. The level of education is related to higher social and economic status in the Nepalese context, as is education itself. A positive attitude towards any kind of development, management practice by the educated people of the village can make it successful and handy. Education is a variable which inhibits/motivates people in development programme. High level of development is possible in regions with high literacy levels (Upadhyay, 2007). The literacy rate of Tanahun district is 73%. The stipulation of schools and campuses are depicted in the table.

Table 3.4

The Educational Institutions of Tanahun District

S.N.	School/Campus	Government	Public	Private	Total
1.	Primary (1-3) class	179		8	187
2.	Primary (1-5) Class	218		20	238
3.	Lower Secondary	54		5	59
4.	Secondary	75		21	96
5.	Higher Secondary	8		4	12
6.	Technical Institution			1	1
7.	Campus		5	2	7

Total	534	5	61	600

Source: District Education Office, Tanahun, 2011

The number of primary schools with classes 1-5 is highest in number with a total of 218 educational institutions. The number of campuses both public and private rests at the lowest with only 7 in number. There is only one technical institution in this district.

Health Facilities

There is a popular Nepali proverb related to health *–ill health and the debt incurred due to bad health are worst forms of human misery*. If the people are physically and mentally well being they will be able to manage their economic and social life effectively and hence prosperity will be a part of their life. Health is also the human right for citizens. Male and female have the right to get the health service. In this regard government and civil society are also responsible to provide health and sanitary facilities to the people. If there is good health there is better life.

Table 3.5

Health Centers of Tanahun District

S.N.	Institutions	Govt.	NGO/INGO	Private	Total
1.	Sub-health Posts	31			31
2.	Health Posts	13			13
3.	Primary Health Centre	1			1
4.	Hospital	2	1	2	5
5.	Nursing home/Research Centre				
	Total	47	1	1	50

Source: District Development Committee, Tanahun, 2011

The table clarifies that there are altogether 50 health institutions in this district with one sub-health posts, 13 health posts, 1 primary health centre, and one hospital. There is no private nursing home or research centre in this district. Compared to the population of the district, the number of health centers is relatively low.

Roadways

Prithvi Highways cross almost the mid part of Tanahun east to west; it is more than 72 K.M. in length. The road to Besisahar-Lamjung area route runs from Dumre Bazar to Gorkha district of western Nepal. From Anbukhaireni Bazaar other village level roads connect various inner parts of the district. Among them Asian Development Bank supported road is the backbone of local economy. The infra-structure of roads is extensive in various parts of the district. It is supporting to the local people and their economy.

Tourism

Tanahun is the potential area for touristic development. Cultural and ecological tourism both are suitable for this area. Tourism plays a vital role in community development. Ecological tourism might turn out to be a blessing for Tanahun as well as Nepal. In course of history, cultural impression and reconciliatory heritage has remained notable and social transformation remains crucial. Scope of participatory biological diversity conservation is endless. Individuals, society, tourist businessmen, government can focus on attracting foreign tourists and promoting development of tourism. The indigenous Magar, Gurung, Darai, Kumal Villages of Tanahun district can plays major role for the enhancement of ecological tourism and vice versa. In future, it is prone to support the national income also.

Religious touristic spots in this district are Chhabdi Baraha (a religious shrine), Shiva Panchayan Mandir, Akala mandir, Dhor Baraha, Basantapur Thanimai, Chhimkeshowri, Bandipur Khadgamai and Mandir Dev Ghat etc. The historical touristic areas are Ghansikuwa, the palace of Tanahunsur Manungkot, Mirlungkot, Kot darbar, Chhimkeshowri lekh, Thaperk, Bhimbad, Gajarkot etc. Bandipur is a popular tourist destination for international tourists. Bandipur Bazaar is situated on a ridge above the Highway town of Dumre, and presents sightseers with an exhilarating mix of history, architecture, incredible views, awe-inspiring caves and unspoiled landscapes. The place as it is now developed as tourism destiny was originally a trade route of India and Tibet. After the migration of ethnic Newar people mainly from Kathmandu, Bhaktapur and Lalitpur regions six generation ago, the place has developed as a densely populated Newar place, whose history is still evident from the traditional houses, temples etc depicting Newari culture. Other touristic areas of the district are Manhu hill which is potential for trekking and paragliding. Likewise, water rafting is suitable in Madi and Seti River. River rafting to Narayan route site visible from Bandipur is moderately illustrious. Main touristic caves of the region are Vyas Gupha, Siddha Gupha, Parasar Gufa, Millennium Gupha and Siddha Gupa which are famous for attracting internal and external tourists.

Social-economic Profile of Kihun Village with Muslim Settlement

Kihun Village Development Committee (V.D.C.) lies in the Southern part of Tanahun district. It takes five hours walking distance and two hours traveling distance by local transportation to reach Kihun V.D.C. from Khairenitar area the adjacent part of Prithwi highway. There is no concrete evidence of history of the settlement of Kihun VDC. It is believed that people were living from the ancient time in this region. Kihun VDC has its own historical and cultural importance. The scholars present different views about the naming of Kihun VDC. Majority of the Magar and Gurung ethnic groups settlements are found in Tanahun and Shyangja district. In local Gurung language the drinking water is called "*Kiu*'. Hence, the word Kihun is derived from the Gurung word '*Kiu*' which means drinking water. Some local people claim that the word Kihun is made by the name of a kind of fruit known as '*Kimba*' or *Kimbu* (in Nepali) mostly found in this area. The fruit normally ripe in spring season in the hilly areas. Kihun is rich in water resources and Kimba fruits. Kihun, the name of VDC was given in 1978. Previously it was called Kihun Badahar Bhanjyang VDC.

Kihun VDC has been crammed by splendid variety of natural beauties and scenario. It is linked with Bhimkali Marga road from Khairenitar, Tanahun. It makes easy to reach the Kihun VDC by local road linkage from Bhimad region. Kihun, one of the forty six V.D.C.s of Tanahun district is at the southern most part of Tanahun and that region belong to *Ilaka* (area) number ten and election constituency no three of this district. The border of Kihun V.D.C is linked with Arunodaya V.D.C in the East and North, Chitrebhanjyang V.D.C of Shyangja district and Gajarkot V.D.C. of Tahahun district in the South.

Satikot, the highest elevation of Kihun lies at 1124 meter (3654 ft) from the sea level. Kihun VDC is located at the Latitude 27 degree 56'23" North and Longitude 83 degree 59'm 08 sec in the East. The landscape is made by terraced sloppy area, hills and small valleys. Satikot hill range extends from north to south elevation at the central part of the VDC.

Enchanting scenes of the terraces, covered by colorful floras, park of different species and birds and running of local springs, streams, are the distinct characteristics of Kihun.

Likewise, Kihun is a harmonious confluence of different ethnic communities having rich cultures and traditions. There prevail the high probabilities that it may be a destination of international and national tourists and holiday makers in future owing to its enchanting daintiness. The huge adjacent rock of Kotthar in adjoining Arunodaya VDC is of round shape and may be a center of tourist attractions in future not only in Arunodaya VDC but in Kihun as well. In broad-spectrum it will be easy to say that Kihun is an emerging village with modern infrastructure development becoming feasible in recent days.

Enchanted with its own historical and cultural importance, Kihun VDC preserves its own social and cultural significance. Different communities like ethnic Magar and Gharti, Hindu Brahmin, Chhetri, Kami, Damai, Sarki, Muslims, and other minor groups reside here. Ethnic Magar are in great majority. Brahmin, Muslim, and low caste Dalits as Kami, Damai are too numerous. Various Hindu festivals are celebrated here every year. Among them *Nag Panchami, Raksha bandhan, Krishnastami, Haritalika Teej, Vijaya Dashami, Deepawali, Haribodhani ekadashi, Maghesakranti, Ramnawami, Baisak purnima, Harelo* (celebrated in the third Tuesday of the month of Bhadra) are the famous. Among the Muslims, *Id, Bakrid and Muharram* are the popular festivals.

Religion is the socio-psychological phenomenon since it inevitably stresses fellowship in the development of teaching and perpetuation of religion insight and knowledge. It is concerned with the common right of all people at all times, regardless of age or status within society. In Kihun VDC as majority of people are following Hinduism except a large population of Muslims in Miyagaon, Hukka area, the hegemony of Hindus is unbridled. There is no population from other religious group beyond the majority Hindu, Buddhism and Islam.

Most of Muslims in Nepal live in the districts of Tarai, but tiny Muslim group have also lived for centuries in Hills as in Kihun. The descendents of Muslims migrated to Kihun from outside especially from Palpa district and other areas in the different historical phases ranging from 250 years to some 30 years. At present Islam is the major religious group of

Miyagaon, Hukka of Kihun VDC, however the stern accomplishment of Hindu philosophy based code and state negligence has restricted Muslims from practicing many of their traditional norms. It is one of the main reasons behind the coldness of the Muslim community and their apathy for inclusion in mainstream society. How far the Muslim masses of Kihun integrate in the mainstream and join the development program under a new political milieu remains blurred but given the same gloomy condition there are high probabilities that they will remain diffident lacking inclusion politically, socially, economically.

Kihun VDC is a confluence of an assortment of caste/ethnic groups living together. Caste is a closed stratum of Hindu society based on heredity that determines its member's prestige, occupation and place of residence and social relationship. Each caste is endogamous and social relations between members of different caste and ethnic group relating cooperative way. They share the ideas in local level issues. People of Kihun VDC join each others in the ceremonies of social fairs and festivals. There is good participation from Islamic community in the social-cultural activities of the village especially in the festivals of Hindus. In this regard there is harmony between Muslims and Hindus. They have the practice of close friendly ties (called "*miteri saino*" in Nepali). At local ceremonies they used to accept the invitation and attend the social and cultural ceremonies and functions. Due to the educational awareness and modernity the rigid caste based relationship and commensality that prevailed between the people in the village in the past is diminishing fast in the present. Collectively the people share the common practices in their own way. The Hindus and the Muslims relationship and brotherhood are becoming more amicable despite religious divergences.

Education is a potent device to augment the human capacity .This is a strong factor for employment, awareness as well as the livelihood of the common people. Education accumulates human knowledge and discharges it when needed. Besides this it helps the social change. The literacy of Tanahun district is 73% and it is 55% in Kihun village. There is one higher secondary school, two lower secondary school, four primary school and two primary level private English medium boarding schools in Kihun village. Badaharbhanjyang is the local hamlet of Kihun, including small business, schools, call (telephone) centers, dispensary, tea shops etc. It is linked with local transportation and other routes. Siddhartha Higher Secondary School located near the market area of Badaharbhanjyang area provides the local intermediate level education for the local students.

Demography

According to the National Population Census of Nepal 2011, the total population of the Kihun village is 3827, in which 1579 are males and 2248 are females. The total population of the village is organized into 917 households. The population and households in each ward and the sample taken from each ward is presented in table. The population of Kihun VDC by caste/ethnic distributions is presented in the table.

Table 3.6

Population by Caste /Ethnic Groups in Kihun Village

S. No.	Caste/Ethnic Groups	Number
1.	Magar	1300
2.	Dalits (so-called low castes)	900
3.	Brahmin	1080
4.	Chhetri	17
5.	Gharti	23
6.	Tamang	18
7.	Hill Muslim(Churoute)	466
8.	Others	23
	Total	**3827**

Population Monograph of Nepal, Central Bureau of Statistics, 2011

Population of female exceeds male in Kihun VDC which is because of the mass migration of young males to foreign countries for jobs. The patriarchic attitude and desire for male child has created a stipulation of a population with female majority. Of the total caste/ethnic based population of Kihun VDC, ethnic Magar are in immense majority. Brahmins are in second position and the Dalits occupy the third position respectively. Hill Muslims (*Churoute*) occupy the fourth position. Among the wards, ward no. five known as Miyagaon, Hukka, is the densely populated Muslim area of Kihun VDC.

Family Structure

Family is a basic kinship unit in its minimal form consisting of a husband, wife and relatives living together or recognized as a social unit including adopted persons. Basically three types of family structures are found in rural Kihun VDC. Nuclear family is the basic unit of family organization composed of a married couple and their offspring's. Joint family is that family which includes three or more generations. Majority of the families are found to be of such type in rural areas of Kihun. Another type of family system i.e. nuclear families are also prevalent in the region which is mainly due to fragmentation of paternal property and the effects of rising modernization trends among the newly married couples.

Health Condition

Human conditions and development activities are influenced by health. If physical and mental condition is resonance human can do everything relating to livelihood and career development. The condition of healthy physical state prevails if the people are physically and mentally well being. Government has the responsibility to facilitate the better health services to their citizens at any cost. If there is the provision of good health service condition there is better and prosperous life. There is a VDC level sub-health post in Kahulebhanjyang locality of Kihun VDC. Local level health services are provided by this Kahulebhanjyang sub-health post and critical cases are referred to Primary Health Care Center (PHCC) at Bhimad, Tanahun which is located at four hours walking distance from Kihun, which is the nearest one. The health status of rural dwellers is not so vibrant. Nutritious intake is very low in rural areas. Balanced diet and nutritious food are rarely available in rural areas. People are living in meager condition, which is the pitiful picture. It is requisite to enhance the awareness programme and productivity program so that to uplift the health condition of the local people. Although subsistence production, most people used to sell their productions rather to consume the local production. It is due the skimpy economic condition of the people which is directing influencing the health status of the people of this village.

Women's status and gender condition

Gender identity is the gender a person self-identifies as. The concept of being a woman is considered to have more challenges, due to society not only viewing women as a social category but also as a felt sense of self, a culturally conditioned or constructed subjective identity. The term *woman* has chronically been used as a reference to and for the female body; this usage has been viewed as controversial by feminists, in the defining a woman. There are qualitative analyses that explore and present the representations of gender; feminists challenge the dominant ideologies concerning gender roles and sex. From the gender perspective, historically women have been getting secondary position in Nepalese society. Even now they have fewer rights to speak about family and social matters in many traditional and literate families. Gradually women's are becoming sensitive for their rights and status has been improving in educated families and such areas. Education is not only the cause for women's growing status. Beyond education, the employment, social awareness, economic opportunity and self consciousness are also playing vital role in bringing changes. Very fewer numbers of women are engaged in economically vibrant job in Kihun VDC. It is because they are lowly educated and are engaged in household chores and even have very less opportunity of decision making in household level and public sector. They have minor role to decide the gap and to decide the number of children. Majority women are suffering with anemia (lack of blood in body) owing to the lack of nutritious food and other health facilities. Social awareness is an important factor for raising status of women. Economic prosperity is a determining factor for enhancing the women status. Here the majority of women want to get education first and then a job to raise their status in the society.

Settlement Pattern

Rural hilly areas of Nepal are sparsely populated in which people farm or depend on natural resources, including the villages and small hamlets that are dispersed. Rural areas are plagued by poverty, with the most vulnerable sectors of the population being women, children and the elderly. The concept of rural development is concerned with rural community, people, poor women, children and men. It emphasizes the increase ability towards the needs and wants. Mainly small farmers, tenants, landless are included in this. **The symptoms of backwardness and poverty in Nepal appear visible in the form of widespread deficiency in diet, shelter and clothing which have been very little affected by the "rhetoric of development". The majority of people living in rural areas of this region suffer from acute poverty. There are thin coverage of institutional credits, rural markets and extension organizations in the rural areas of Kihun VDC. The rural scenario of Kihun VDC calls for greater emphasis on**

rural development. While conversing on rural populace of Kihun VDC it is necessary to address:

- Social development in areas such as education and health
- Local democracy and development: to ensure service delivery
- The role of national and provincial governments in defining the needs of the local people
- Local economic development efforts and rural livelihoods
- Social sustainability by highlighting people's constitutional rights
- Rural development in partnership with different agencies
- Safety, security, welfare and legal issues, the rights of children and settlements.
- Peoples genuine problems of day to day life.
- Settlement pattern

Embedded with settlement pattern, household signifies a group of persons starting a home or living space, who aggregate and share their incomes, as evidenced by the fact that they regularly take meals together-the common cooking-pot definition. The settlement pattern of Kihun VDC is determined by the location of land. Somewhere there is the compact type of settlement and somewhere it is scattered. There is mixed type of population in Kihun. Houses are made in terraced landscape. Basically the local settlements are made of a cluster of 18 to 20 houses. The houses are two or three floor (storey) and single storey depending on economic condition of the house owner. Local materials like mud, stone, bamboo, wood, slate and straw are used. Especially three storey houses are made by economically rich people. Rooms are made in two rows. Such rooms are used for guest's residence. The upper floor is used for storage of food grains.

The ground floor is used for the purpose of kitchen, worshipping the God, and keeping the vessels. Domestic animals are kept in separate places like animal shed and the crop store room (called *dhansar* in Nepali). Dhansar is used for two purposes the lower floor is used for keeping animals and the second floor is for residential purposes or keeping hay, straw and fodder for animal.

Dress Pattern

Village people wear local dresses. Women wear sari and blouse (called *sari-*

choli in Nepali), piece of cloth wrapped at waist called *patuki* in Nepali, shawl called *pachhaura*, a piece of cloth used as lower garment called *lungi* etc. Different ornaments are used in nose by piercing nose called *phuli, bulanki, madwaari.* Earring, watch, and ring are also used widely by rural women. In a semi-feudal Nepalese rural society, there is a high value of ornaments. Rich people especially women use a lot of gold ornament which is a symbol of prosperity and affluence. For the poor it is the silver ornaments or even goes without it. The dress pattern of this village is changing according to time. The young and educated people are wearing modern dress whereas old people still cling to traditional dresses. Old Muslim males usually wear a kind of lower garment called *lungi* and the young people use the western dresses.

Occupations

It is astringent veracity that Nepal is entangled in an assortment of social, economic and political tribulations amidst the rhetoric of *Loktantra* (Democracy) and *Samabesi* (Inclusion). Preponderance of urban as well as rural dwellers is deprived of basic, physical and social-economic amenities and is in paucity. In this village also a limited number of people are involved in government and private jobs. Some people are involved in petty business and foreign services. Majority of people are involved in agriculture. Unemployment is preparing the ground for migration of youth to abroad.

The Muslim settlement Miyagaon, Hukka of Kihun VDC is located in ward no 5 in the Eastern lap of Satikot hill. Miyagaon is a blending of diverse landscape. It is located at the Southern part of Kihun VDC. Selling the bangles and cosmetic goods has been their traditional family occupation. However, at the present only the single old man is found to be practicing the traditional occupation of bangle selling as a vendor. Occupational trend of selling bangles and cosmetics as vendors is changing. Now most of the Muslims are engaged in agricultural activities, jobs abroad, exchange and selling the animals (like goat, bull, cows, buffaloes etc), teaching, fancy shop business etc.

Land and Land Use Pattern in Kihun

The land of the VDC can be divided into terraced land called *Pakho bari* in local language and low lands or paddy areas called *besi khet* locally. The low lands are in the region of the foothills and can be irrigated by rivers and streams. The dry land (*bari*) can be further categorized, according to the types of soil found, those with red soil and gray soil. The gray soil can immerse abundant water while the red soil becomes slippery after rainfall. From the agricultural point of view, the gray soil can grow crops with little water, while the red soil needs more water. The dry land (*Pakho*) in the VDC, apart from the land in the vicinity of Satikot and Kot thar hills, is not stony and is considered good for crops.

The total land area of the Kihun VDC is approximately 956 hectares. Of this land, 775 hectares is agricultural land, 20 hectares residential area, and 10.1 hectares grazing pasture land. The rest 151 hectares is covered with forest. The data, however, should be evaluated with some caution, as there are also private forest registered as agricultural land (esp. the adjacent part of agricultural land) private agriculture land in the name of individuals (locally it is called *lohose*) or local peoples land.

Based on land use survey, the lands are categorized in four different types, such as

a) Fertile land *(known as abal)*

b) Semi-fertile *(doyam)*

c) Low fertile *(sim)* and

d) Barren land *(chahar)*

Temperature and Rainfall

Basically, the Middle Western part of Nepal is influenced by semi-temperate (moderate type of climate). Especially this type of climate is found in sloppy areas, *bhanjyang*, hills and small valleys of rural areas. Some areas of *Tar* (unirrigated land) and *Besi* (low land) are influenced by sub-tropical climate. The maximum temperature remains 31degree Celsius (87 degree Fahrenheit) in June/ July and minimum temperature remains 8 degree Celsius (46 degree Fahrenheit) in winter season. The maximum mean temperature remain 19.66 degree Celsius and minimum 11.83 degree Celsius. Due to the cause of environmental change and global warming, the present climatic condition of this area has been also influenced.

Kihun VDC enjoys semi-temperate (moderate type of climate), and sub-tropical climate. The south-east monsoon is, as in other areas of the country, the major climate influence, providing water to the two important cereal crops rice and millet in the village. The low lands (besi) experience sub-tropical climate while the higher regions are cooler with mid and cool temperate climates.

Rivers and Natural Resources

The VDC lies at an altitude of approximately 700 meters to 1500 meters. The Satikot (Kihun VDC) and Kotthar hills (Arunodaya VDC) which lie from the north-east to the south, divide the VDC into almost two halves. The Rahu Khola (also called the Gopha Khola and Salagdi Khola), which starts at Arunodaya VDC, flows in the east and south of the VDC. The Rahu Khola separates Kihun from Arunodaya and Ghiring-Sundhara VDCs. The Kulung Khola, starting from chitre Bhanjyang, flows in the west and south of the VDC and separates Kihun from Gajarkot VDC and Shyangja district. The two rivers encircle the VDC from the east, west, and south before joining together to flow into the Kali Gandaki River. The two rivers provide irrigation facilities to the low land (*besi*) on the both sides of river or the catchments areas. Besides these two rivers, there are other streams like Ubdi Khola, Thulokhet Khola and Charangdi Khola. The Charangdi Khola forms a precipitous fall-called the Charangdi falls-before joining the Kulang Khola. There are, in addition to these streams, also wells and other traditional waters sources in the VDC. These rivers, wells, and other water sources shrink during the dry season, although they do not completely dry up. These water sources increases during the monsoon and, along with the other water sources sprout during the period, provide abundant water for drinking and irrigation. Most of the land is occupied by rapidly mounting population for the purpose of agriculture and settlement. Accordingly, the land use pattern is rapidly changing. There is vast change in previous condition of the forest and the present vast forest area has been converted into agricultural land or settlement locations.

4

SOCIAL ETHNOGRAPHIC STATUS OF THE MUSLIMS

Nepal is a cultural mosaic; indisputably a pluralistic and multicultural society amid discriminatory state machinery which is Kathmandu centered and dominated by Aryan *Pahadiya* (hill dwelling) higher castes elites. Owing to egocentrism of higher caste Hindu Brahmin-Chhetri rulers (known as *Khas* rulers in Nepali language) located in capital city, people residing in diverse parts of Nepal has been continuously discriminated. The non-Aryan ethnic groups, Terai-Madhesh dwellers, far western Karnali region caste/ethnicities, Muslims etc are the worst sufferers. All the political movements that happened in Nepal so far 1951, 1990, 2006, had the prime focus on the elimination of elitism, suppressions, discriminations etc. Nevertheless, after all political revolutions, the situation remains more or less the same owing to which Nepal is continuously facing quandary and is poised to deal with fierce challenges from excluded groups and counter revolutions in future from internal feudal, brokers, corrupt bureaucracy, hill dwelling high caste *Khas* (Brahman, Chhetri) elites and their unitary state based egocentrism.

With the establishment of republican democracy and development of capitalism, the voices of marginalized historically suppressed groups are noticeable. At first such voices were seen in developed capitalist centers of cities, but with the advent of Peoples war by Maoist in 1996, awareness spread to remote regions of the country. With the establishment of republican democracy and the development of capricious capitalism, the voices of marginalized groups are on the raise. At first such voices were seen in developed capitalist centers of cities, but with the advent of Peoples war by Maoist insurgents since 1996, awareness spread to remote regions of the country. The awareness level of Muslim masses is also increasing at a snail's pace.

The Muslim community of Miyagaon, Hukka with a distinct culture, a distinct religious group has been incommodious with innumerous social-economic tribulations and hindrances in day-to-day life. With the religious and cultural image of untouchables (called *malecha* in Nepali) creating social stigma and different sorts of barriers, which they are supposed to counter in their daily life, life is not a bed of roses but full of thorns with diverse sorts of quandary to confront. Nevertheless, their society is a bounded, self-functioning and self-maintaining system that maintains its equilibrium in the face of an uncomfortable and hostile environment. For their society's survival its various social processes are meshing smoothly together to meet the system's needs. The vital question is *how does Muslim community meeting its needs?* Each institution of this community, practice and process is seen as performing more of less a function that meets a societal need and thereby helping to maintain the society's structure or equilibrium. The social, cultural and economic institutions of Muslim community are playing their roles to keep sustainable the minority Muslim society encircled by majority Hindus.

It was deduced from respondents that different groups of Muslims came from Lhasa and settled in Basantapur village of Tanahun and later migrated to Sundhara, Gajarkot VDC of Tanahun and finally settled in Miyagaon, Hukka of Kihun VDC. The migratory history of Muslims in this VDC goes back to about two hundred fifty years ago, according to the local respondents. Some of their ancestors came from Rampur village of Palpa district of western Nepal and other areas. Basically the purpose of entry was a search for better life, commerce and security. The groups were mainly Tibetan and Kashmiri Muslims. Other Muslim groups also came from Kashmir and settled in the rugged hills of Kihun. In the historical phase, Muslims groups were invited by Shah and Sen Kings for the purpose to supply the butyl or cosmetic materials in the *durbar* (palace), to make the weapons, military trainings as well as Muslim method of health treatment. They were Bihari, Bengali and Awadhi Muslims. The Muslims also appeared as invitee for fulfilling various tasks, e.g. making weapons as guns and explosives for the kings, making beads, ornaments, selling cosmetics, bangles etc. Areas like Sataun and Nuwakot of Syangja district, Kaski, Lamjung, Gorkha districts and Sen rulers ruled historical Principality (during the 18 and 19 century) of Tanahun are the other main hilly regions in the Gandaki region of western Nepal where Muslim arrivals settled. Nevertheless, hill Muslims of Hukka, Kihun are distinct from Kathmandu and Terai Muslims because of cross-marital relationship with local women of hills, local cultural influences, of *Sanskritization* process, physical structure, local language and other local cultural impacts. The hill Muslims called *Miyas* of Miyagaon, Hukka reserves their own identities with spatial territory, *Miya* language as a mother tongue, the word *Miya* is used for the identity of clan, bangle traders. Nevertheless at present the term *Miya* is used to denote the Muslims and there are three mosques at present here. Traditionally these Muslims are bangle makers and cosmetic traders. However, at present a good number of the hill Muslims of Hukka are agricultural farmers and hardly any are involved in traditional occupations.

Social Status of Muslims of Miyagaon, Hukka

Social status processes are embedded with the notion of development. Despite its universal currency and exhortatory prospective, in some ways, *development embedded with issues of social statuses* reminds one of the stories of the elephant and the six blind men. In the Nepalese context development is somehow holy, uplifting and attractive. It is, however, also mysterious. The object is subjectively perceived and the totality of subjectivities does not add to an objective description and/or assessment. Instead the totality becomes more and more bizarre, unfamiliar and abstract. An aim which is itself inexplicable, in turn, inspires a mode of practice which is essentially misleading. Underdevelopment in Nepal, in fact, has a long history whose roots lie in the continuous, if uneven, process of social exclusions. The Nepali state alliance composed of the state class, i.e., the proponents of the various formal political-organizational systems that have been created and lived under. The town-hazed *middle class*, the feudal landed interests bourgeoisie and the socially excluded marginalized are largely offshoots of this process and they are the main link through which the process of exclusion have been sustained and underdevelopment reproduced. The capital city of lavishness and political power Kathmandu valley had been enjoying a highly developed agrarian-artisan-trading culture at least from the seventh century onwards with a high social status of the elites. For the common people, status signifies a position, rank or grading of both male and female below an accepted status. United Nations has defined the status in the context of peoples access to economic resources, knowledge and political power, as well as their personal autonomy in the process of decision making inside the home and outside in the society.

Based on the notion of *status,* Social-economic status is a system of stratification, a combination of various social and economic indexes of rank that are used in research studies. The term often used to deal with stratification in a society without the need of the assumption that there are distinct social classes. Social characteristics (family background, education, values, prestige of occupation, etc.) and economic status (income) are combined into SES (Social-economic Status) rating. Age, gender, caste and ethnicity, religion, family background, educational status, marital status etc are social aspects and occupation, income, living standard etc are the economic aspects (Dictionary of Sociology, 1999). When Miyagaon, Hukka's Muslims status is analyzed in this light, the depiction is generally depressing for all, but in the context of girl child, as Nepal is a rigidly patriarchic and semi-feudalistic society, its worst. Here girl's condition is ominous in every aspect of life. Thousands of years old semi-feudalistic patriarchal agriculture based society has deteriorated the status of girls owing to which they are subordinate to males virtually in every aspect of their life. It is not only girls but also males are backward in all aspects of the society. To trace their status, it is vital to ponder on occupation, household income; types of houses, health and sanitation that are the economic aspects and health, sanitation, gender disparities, education as social aspects.

Economy acts as the mirror that depicts the social status of an individual. In sociology and anthropology, ***social status*** is the honor or prestige attached to one's position in society (one's social position). The stratification system, which is the system of distributing rewards to the members of society, determines social status. Social status, the position or rank of a person or group within the stratification system, can be determined two ways. One can earn their social status by their own achievements, which is known as achieved status, or one can be placed in the stratification system by their inherited position, which is called ascribed status (*en.wikipedia.org/wiki/**Social_status.2007***). Likewise, social and cultural structures of the society are important themes in sociological and anthropological studies. They are very closely related to the issues of growth and development. Unless and until the cultural and social structures are not comprehended, it is not easy to solve any kind of problem or any kind of development-allied issues. The society is a social web of social relationship, human behaviors and their consequences. Generally, society is a system where people live with their culture in a fixed geographical environment, along with a fixed social structure; social barriers and well-defined social relationships. The conception of culture is undeniably influential in shaping concepts and practices related to physical environment. Social and cultural phenomenon's have differing roles to play in this complex process and therefore must be researched separately. Culture shapes or determines people's use of surroundings. At the same time different components of culture, in different conditions and circumstances and at different time manipulate all behavior pattern. Human behavior is multi-potential, at any point in the life cycle of individuals the number of possible responses to a given situation is in fact constrained by previous learning, standardized responses, and conventional values. Still, it is never possible to rule out the role and value of cultural and social structure in influencing behavior of Muslims related to development and other activities. Likewise, the role of economy in shaping the destiny of Muslim community can't be refuted.

Prior to the instigation of any kind of development programme it is prerequisite that local social and cultural structure, people's sentiments should be taken into proper contemplation. People are themselves sensitive subject of study, they are self conscious having individual personality, motives, emotions, sentiments, norms and values and because of this, they are self capable of choosing their own course of action or in deciding when to participate and how to participate in any kind of development or resources management activity and the courses of actions and activities are to a great extent determined by the social and cultural structure. Cultural rituals used to serve not only religious functions but also serve social and environmental functions not only in this Muslim area of Hukka but in other areas also. The ethnography of Muslim community is such that they follow same systems (embedded with Islamic creed), which are practiced by dominant hill people of other groups---both Hindus and Buddhists according to the norms of their religion.

Given the liveliness of social and cultural structure and people's prime role in development, it is imperative to comprehend the social and cultural structure of Muslims of Hukka. The social and cultural structure of Muslims of Hukka is found to be highly drenched in traditional Muslim norms and values as well as other Hindu groups because of the fact that majority of the inhabitants of this region are Hindus owing to which gender and traditional concepts are very strict here in both Muslim and Hindu community. There is also the intricate co-operative feeling among the Muslims and Hindus. They call each other's to their local fairs and festivals. They are closely tied with the congenial ties. Owing to which their society and culture has been *Sanskritized* to some extent, which is reflected in their behaviors and in their efforts for participation in various activities, related to economic and social enhancement.

Social indicators covering a wide range of subject-matter fields are vital for creating consequences on development. Measures to indicate social progress, *social indicators,* have been discussed at length in this current study, and the importance of economic indicators regarded undisputed. Likewise, empirical measures of cultural status in comparison also remain imperative. This study attempted to illustrate how an integrated framework combining social and cultural indicators of development may be applied to measure social status of the Muslims.

In the context of Miyagaon, Hukka the social indicators depicting social status are as follows:

Family Structure

Family size is the number of people living in the same home as the members of the same unit. This includes relatives and other household members. There are not equal numbers of family member in every household and the family size is different. Mostly, there are large family sizes; because of the verity that Muslims do not practice family planning i.e. permanent or temporary. The family size of Muslim households is depicted in the table.

Table 4.1

Family Structure

Family Size	Households Number	Family Number
1	1	1
2	5	10
3	1	3

4	6	24
5	10	50
6	10	60
7	6	42
8	5	40
9	6	54
10	3	30
11	2	22
12	3	36
13	1	13
14	2	28
15	23	0
23	12	3
Total	**64**	**466**

Source: Field Survey, 2010

According to the table, family sizes vary sharply. The distribution of family members is one to twenty three members. Among 64 households, large family structure is common in many households. 10 families have five or six member's family structure among 64 households. One household has only one member among the 64 households of Hukka, 6 households has nine members in the study area. 10 member households are three in number.

Moreover, the ratio of one household has seven members in that settlement. It is deduced from the above table that there exists the high number of family members in Hukka with an average population of 7 members in average Muslim family. It means the family size of Muslims of Miyagaon, Hukka, is 7 per household which is larger than any other caste and ethnic groups of Nepal. In total there are 64 households and the total Muslim population is 466. Only one household has single member and another one has three. Two families have 15 members and one has 23 members. Muslim houses have been built in cluster and has limited space with limited number of rooms in their house and maximum number of houses has only one room in the space of ground floor. On the other hand, by the distribution of family members, the sizes of houses are very small with one room for their every activity, i.e. their kitchen, bedroom and store all is in a single room. Consequently, Muslims life style is incredibly stiff due to congested accommodation in small houses crowded with a huge family size.

Built in traditional Nepali hill style, the first floor of the house is used for the purpose of keeping food grains. The domestic cattle's are keep in separate sheds. Regarding the condition of houses, 43 houses are permanently made by the use of the local construction materials as thatch, hay and stone. 21 houses are temporarily built. Only 4 toilets are made permanently, 23 are temporary and 37 household members use open toilet in the bushes and forest nearby. There is no regular facility of tap drinking water; mostly local people use the local water resources from the local water sources called *Pani Ko Mul* in local language. Relatively, the condition depicts the low social status of the Muslims of Hukka.

Family Size, Children, Elderly Population and Insinuation on Social Status and Gender

By and large, huge family size and economically inactive dependent members are the contributing factors responsible for the lower social status of the Muslims. Females are the victims of large family size, as they have to bear extra responsibilities of children and old people. Status is not similar everywhere and in all groups as women's relative status varies from one group to another. Owing to patriarchal and Islamic traditions, the social status of male in Muslim male is relatively better than that of females. From economic insulation, Muslim households have big structure hence it is very difficult for these households to feed all members. At the same time, there is no regular occupational stability among the Muslims. Although the Nepalese constitution offers, man and women equal educational opportunities, many social, economic, and cultural factors, Muslim religious taboos contributed to lower level of educational attainment for all Muslims. Muslims folks are trapped in a vicious circle imposed by the capitalist and patriarchic society owing to which there have been very little socio-cultural changes. Socio-cultural change relates to local quality of life and sense of belonging to native place and *we feelings*. Positive change in the quality of life will be possible only with personal income increase that helps to improve living standards for those directly involved, nevertheless it is not so with the Muslims of Hukka. Negative changes in the quality of life is proving detrimental to people's needs resulting in the loss of authenticity and inaccuracy in interpretation, alienation and loss of cultural identity, displacement of traditional residence etc.

The condition of womenfolk in Muslim community is appalling and it is fading at a rapid pace. They are to look after children as mother, to look after homes as homemakers and to look after the elderly people especially father and mother -in -laws. Side by side, they are compelled to go and work outside for subsistence agricultural works to support the family economically. Women in large size family have high burdens of internal (household chores) and external (agricultural) works dichotomies and high the dichotomies, low the participation of the women in social and development related activities of the community and the village.

As the sentiments of majority of Muslims are based on a Muslim religious system, a women's identity is formed through marriage ties; 'adherence to duty and obedience' are held as high virtues. Following the organizing principles of the superiority of men, a Muslim woman is ranked according to her relationship with men and given lower status because of her inferior ritual purity and this has been influencing their participation in decision-making-both internal and external. It is also deduced that differences between males/females in their priority for social-economic development are largely different- that is culturally/socially determined.

Amidst social, economic and household burdens, women in Muslim families are discriminated against and lag far behind in many areas, barring a few exceptions, mainly because of long-held social and cultural structure and attitude. In Muslim community, where economic development has not benefited all, Modernization theory with emphasis on the market, or an economic-planning approach in which state intervention is thought to be needed to remove obstacles hindering women's progress by bringing industrial revolution, has been futile. The scenario is of poverty-stricken masses, with an under-developed commercial base in Muslims settlement that has deteriorated the situation. Owing to this, questions are being raised about the viability of modernization approach to development and in upgrading the status of Muslim women. At the level of the national government in Nepal, there is a lack of explicit policy and programme formulation to reduce gender disparities; at the community level, social and religious norms and taboos continue to prevail and constrain the activities of women; and at the household level, there is often an overt discrimination against women in the Muslim's settlement. The consequence is that the status of women in Muslims remains low despite the rhetoric of *democracy and inclusion* in urban pockets.

Even, in urban areas of Nepal where the so called *modern* society prevails, women suffer from social, cultural, economic and political prejudices, and as heads of households they have to bear the full conventional roles with the added responsibility of household and production management. Among the Muslims of Hukka to some extent men have benefited from expanded educational and employment opportunities, however, women's relative status has probably been dilapidated owing to the mounting population pressure, producing more and more children, children nurture, responsibility of taking care of large family, searching for alternative economic opportunities etc. Here the nature of gender bias has been exacerbating through the extent of household poverty. The incidence of male involved in domestic violence and domination, resulting in psychological depression and dependency syndrome among women is growing high among the women of Muslim community. Muslim women's subordination is a consequence of the development of patriarchy, private property and that a successful struggle and the demise of religion based patriarchy are therefore required before gender inequities can be changed. Marxist thinkers have put their energies into the struggle against capitalism, rather than trying to attack patriarchy, which they argue is merely an outgrowth of the capitalist system. Given this authenticity, in the milieu of the women of Muslims, it is deduced that under the yoke of Islam religion and pre-dominant patriarchy, womenfolk are to suffer and their social-economic status continues to deteriorate amidst the rhetoric of democracy, progress and advancements.

Amid the prevailing religious orthodoxy, caste/ethnicity and conventions ridden customary society, discriminations against poor and women are rampant in the Nepali society among the Hindus and other ethnic and religious groups. The dimensions of the society intertwined with discriminatory issues is an issue of great sociological and anthropological interest as Nepalese social-economic system is a product of various social, cultural and historical processes based on hegemony and ostracism. Social stratifications are responsible for several social, cultural and political deformities at present and the Muslims are the direct victims.

In Nepal, it is seen from the researches conducted by INGO "SAVE THE CHILDREN" (1993) that more the region is developed economically and socially, low the rate and degree of ethnicity, religion and caste based discriminations. On the other hand, if the region is backward and less developed the cases of discrimination is high. In the context of the Miyagaon, Hukka as the Muslim people are illiterate and less aware towards their rights, it is definite that in this area status and gender based stratification is acute. The main determining force behind this is the regions level of economic development, social and other factors, education, impact of rural background, religious dogma etc.

During the field study, it was reported to researcher that not only the Muslims even the lower caste Hindu Dalits and low class people were treated in discriminatory way and they themselves sat apart because they are accustomed to this habit. The oppressed are not in a position to protest against the injustice because of mass illiteracy, century old suppression and the fatalistic feudal notion of *patron-client relationship* that prevails in Nepali society. The higher caste Hindu groups of Kihun VDC treat the Muslims as untouchables. Hence, religion based *hegemony* of the mainstream people is the factor of discrimination between the Hindus and Muslims.

Rise of *Culture of Poverty*, Backwardness and Conflict Nexus

Sociologists believe that the stage of acute poverty, backwardness and suppression for a long time, used to produce a *culture of poverty*-- that is a culture shared by the poor and the backwards of the same group. Oscar Lewis first used the term culture of poverty in 1968 while conducting study in Central America. The culture of poverty, thus, is a design or a style for living, which is transmitted from one generation to next and which influences all aspects of individual's life. In the case of Hukka, religious, ethnic and class based stratifications and the possession of the social status of religious alien has imparted adverse effects on the life Muslims owing to which a *culture of poverty* has developed among the lower class Muslims affecting all aspects of their life, their mind-set, psychology and activities. Such has been the affects of *culture of poverty* that the low class Muslims beyond meek protest to researcher during the course of interviews, rarely protest openly to the suppression, exploitations and discrimination of the high-class people from both Muslim and Hindu communities. The culture of poverty has developed among the low class, a strong present-time orientation with relatively little ability to defer gratification and a sense of surrender and fatalism but with a hidden sentiment to oppose and go in resistance to discriminations. Hence a nexus is traceable between religious discriminations, rise of *Culture of Poverty*, backwardness and probable conflict.

Religious Traditions and Internal Conflicts

According to Dictionary of Sociology (1999), direct and conscious struggle between individuals or groups for the same goal is defined as *conflict*. Defeat of the opponent is seen as essential for achieving the goal. In conflict (unlike competition), opponents are primarily oriented towards each other rather than towards the object they seek. In fact, because of the development of strong feelings of hostility, the achievement of the goal may at times be considered secondary to opponents defeat. In addition, conflict is intermittent rather than continuous. According to the Encyclopedia of Sociology (2003), conflict theory is the Sociological perspective that focuses on tension, competitions and division in society. It assumes that no society is devoid of conflicts of interest and that in the process of struggling for scarce and valuable resources, groups develop strategies to maximize their rewards and minimize their losses. Likewise, conflict types also vary. There are various types of divergences and occasional conflicts that erupt in Muslim community, for example; the argument used to be over the differences to look and to evaluate the *Id-Ka-Chand* (evaluation of moon's position based on lunar calendar determining the celebration of Id-festival) between Muslim groups. In 2012, when the researcher was in Miyagaon, Hukka, a conflict erupted between two factions of Muslims regarding the evaluation and looking of the *Id-Ka- Chand.* The conflict was prone to take a bloody form when it was timely averted by the interference of senior fellows and some senior politicians of Muslim community. Few respondents accepted of the reality of conflicts regarding economic and other social conflicts both intra (within the Muslim community) and inter (between Muslim and Hindu community). Amid the *culture of poverty,* internal strife's and reporting of discriminations are common; however, the situation is not out of control. The open and sharp intra (Muslims vs. Muslims) and inter (Muslims vs. Hindus) conflict has not occurred openly so far now in Hukka however in future it may take dangerous shape if misused by vested interests of politicians.

Educational Status

Education is the diffusion of knowledge by either formal or informal techniques. The notion of socialization and learning are related to, in fact often inseparable from, the concept of education. Although education is often thought of in terms of schooling (formal education), effective training for the individual role as both a group member and an autonomous person is a constant process. The main function of the educative process is to pass down knowledge from generation to generation- a process that is essential to the development of culture. Formal education is primarily designed to inculcate crucial skills and values central to the survival of the society or to those who hold effective power. Inherent in education, in all periods of man's history, is a stimulus to creative thinking and action, which accounts in part for culture change, culture change itself being a powerful stimulus to further innovation. Education is one of the most imperative factors determining social, economic, and educational status. Qualification is also the most important silhouette for better job and employment. Education contributes to personal and professional development, bringing opportunities in life. Education is supposed to be a path not only for a better living but also for prestige is a bright future of every human being. Although education is vital element of human development, the literacy rate of Nepal is in the range of 70%. Over 30% people are illiterate yet in present day Nepal.

Although education in the Nepalese context may be playing prime role in strengthening social relationships, there exists no trepidation that education is an important attribute for the development of human personality and leadership skill so that to work in any kind of development or management works. The level of education is related to higher social and economic status, as is education itself. A positive attitude towards any development practice by the educated people of the village can make it handy. Education is a variable, which inhibits/motivates people in development programmes. Hence, the nature and acclaim of *--literate vs. illiterate* is vital to be comprehended for the comprehension of socio-ethnographic status of the people. For the masses in Hukka, education is a medium for social enhancement though education is not a privilege; it is the right of every child. For them education is essential to become a free human being, so that one can be liberated from all sorts of backwardness, mistreatment and oppression. An educated child is the greatest treasure. Education is important, as it gives imagination, creativity, and energy. It is a source of empowerment and the indicator of discrimination. It is clear that investment in education is a sustainable investment, which has returns in overall social-economic status that are the greatest resource of any country. Although Muslim parents are aware of the importance of education, many children are deprived of of basic rights of education. In the context of Miyagaon, Hukka, the educational status of Muslims has been presented in the table:

Table 4.2

Educational Status of Muslims

Educational Status	**Number**	**Percent (%)**
Illiterate	79	17
Literate	363	78
Matriculation	14	3
Intermediate	6	1.20
Bachelors Level	4	0.8
Total	466	100.0

Source: Field Survey, 2012

It is an irony that the numbers of literate people is high among 466 respondents. The literate people are 363 in number with a percentage of 78. Nevertheless, illiterate people are also high in number. Their number is 79(17%). Illiterate means those people who cannot read and write at all and have no knowledge what is meant by education. Here literate means those people who can read and write or those having matriculation pass certificates, Intermediate and Bachelors level education. In Hukka Miyagaon the matriculation/SLC (School Leaving Certificate) passed people's number are 14 (3%). In addition, the intermediate level passed are six (1.20%) in number and the Bachelors level passed are only 4(0.8%). There is no Master degree holder in Muslim community. Likewise, single Staff Nurse and single Engineer are in technical sector in the whole Muslim community of Hukka. It is deduced that the literacy rate is comparatively better in Muslim settlement in Hukka but this has not been able to raise the social and economic status of the people which is an irony in itself. One of the possible reasons is practice of the strict dogma of Islamic credo and the religion based discriminations. The existing scenario of illiterate people is also not a good symptom and it is prone that this percentage of illiterate people is certain to influence the social-economic status of the Muslim community. At the present, the Muslim children attend *Madrassas (*Muslim religious school), government Secondary school or Higher Secondary School. *Madrassas* lacks quality education, lacks government support and many of the *madrassas* are developing slowly into centers for the dissemination of radical Islamic thoughts that may create probable threat to the security situation of the whole region. There are allegations that Pakistan's military secret service Inter Services Intelligence (ISI) is providing financial support to *madrassas* and playing its invisible role in stirring up the sentiments of innocent Muslims of this remote region by provoking their fundamentalist dogma. The remoteness of the region is proving to be a safe haven for the Muslim terrorists also who are wanted in India. In 2013 one notorious Muslim terrorist responsible for bombing in different cities of India was apprehended from Pokhara city which is in the vicinity of Miyagaon, Hukka. Hence, the logic that Islamic fundamentalism supported by Islamic terrorism may be a serious threat to the security of the whole region in future, seems realistic.

Distribution of Children by School Attendance

The total Muslim population in Miyagaon, Hukka is 466. A number of students attended schools and *Madrassas* whereas some are irregular in school. School dropout is also high; students left their school for various reasons. School dropout is owing to parental negligence, poor economic conditions, lack of awareness, cattle caring etc. It is deduced that the children above the age of four years go to school and the children below that age do not go to school. Children not going to school are those students who left schools or are school dropouts and some children has not attained the necessary age to attend the school. Some children left their school and they do labor works and cattle rearing but their number is only few. It means maximum number of children goes to school and only few children left their school. However, highly educated people's number is very few in Muslim community. More children left their school under matriculation at the age of fifteen or sixteen owing to grim economic condition of the family. They go to Gulf countries for as laborers for jobs.

Types of Schools

The purpose of education may be to instill discipline and respect or to give everyone an equal chance to broaden their intellectual and emotional life. Some people would say it provides a small minority with an intensive, high equality process of intellectual stimulation until they are adult, and gives the poorer majority a lower quality basic education until they are in their adolescence. Marxists believe education operates to reproduce the capitalist class system and to produce an indoctrinated worker to work for stabilizing the capitalist order of society. In the Nepalese context, education is producing unemployed youth supposed to work as laborers in gulf countries. It is becoming luxurious day by day in Nepalese context where there has been the burgeoning of private schools in the cities in the recent days.

There are three types of schools in Miyagaon. One is government, another is semi-government Muslim schools called *madrassas* and last type is private school. The government school is supported by the government through District Education Office. Muslim School *Madrassas are* semi-government but lacks apposite support from the government. The governments schools are attended by common people's children, rich people's children attend private English Boarding schools which are expensive and unaffordable for the majority poor. Many of the religious minded Muslims send their children to *madrassas*. In Nepal NGO (Non-government organization) culture is on rise. Numerous childcare centers are running in cities with the help of the NGOs. But such types of centers are not accessible in Hukka. It means that there is no child care center in Muslim settlement.

Parents Encouragement for Children to Study at Home

In Muslim settlement, rare numbers of people are well educated. It means less numbers of people are highly educated. The education of parent and their encouragement for their children to study at home is important for educational achievement. Home is the first school of children and *mother is the first teacher*, but in the context of Muslims, many parents are illiterate or are not well educated. Hence, many parents give first priority to *Madrassas* and second priority to general school. Owing to the burly agricultural tradition children are engaged in domestic and agricultural activities hence they give less precedence to school education. It is hopelessness, frustration and the home environment of children and the behavior of parents that shapes their education at school. The similar penchant is prevailing in the Muslim settlement. The primary data collected from the field helped in justifying this logic. (34%) parents encourage their children to study at home, and (24%) are not encouraging their children to study at home and rest (18%) parents asked their children to study self because they cannot teach and guide their children but they realize the importance of home study. Moreover, 24 percent people do not response about it. The data reveals that only 34 percent people do encourage for their children and as the preponderance parents are illiterate and lowly educated hence they are not in a position to suggest and guide to their children. Many of the Muslim guardians are longing to tutor their children but they cannot tutor hence are compelled to arrange self-study for their children at home. They cannot handle their children or tutor in the case children are studying at English boarding schools. Owing to illiteracy, lack of quality education on the part of guardians, low level of awareness, they are not in a position to encourage and guide their children to study at home consequently their children are emaciated in classrooms compared to the children of other groups.

Adult Literacy Program

Adult education is a specialized aspect of education that includes a variety of programs involving the instruction of persons over legal age outside the system of formal education. From its beginning in Great Britain in the 1800's the movement for adult instruction has become worldwide (Encyclopedia of Sociology, 2003). Magill (2003) reveals in the Encyclopedia of Sociology that the phrase *Adult Education* was first used by Thomas Pole, an English physician, in his book *A History of the Origin and Progress of adult Schools* published in 1816. Pole was concerned that adults should be able to read and write in order to read the Bible. From this beginning in Britain, adult education has spread throughout the countries of the world. It has developed along several different lives, coalescing into four broad categories: adult literacy training and retraining Programs, returning students, and continuing education. The actual process of teaching adults is a sub-discipline of education called *andragogy* that is important for illiterate adult people. The National Census of 2011 clarifies that illiterate people are little above 30% in Nepal, majority of who are the adults. In the Muslim settlement of Miyagaon, Hukka the literate peoples number is 387 (83%) but 79 (17%) illiteracy is also not a negligible figure. Majority of illiterate in Muslim settlement are the adults. But, the gloomy facet of adult literacy is that the adult literacy program is seasonally and partially available in this settlement and there is no permanent availability of adult literacy programme. Illiterate adult people can take part in adult education programme partially for a fixed period of time. Few people took the advantages of adult literacy program after migration to elsewhere outside Hukka area. As a whole, it is deduced that adults are illiterate in this settlement owing to the absence of permanent adult literacy programme.

Health Status

Health is an integral part of the society. Without adequate levels of health, society's member cannot productively contribute to its growth and development. Different societies emphasize in health care in different ways. Less developed societies tend to have lower levels of health and less advanced health care system than more developed societies. The health status denotes health stipulation of Muslims connoted by certain concerns.

Health Checkup or the Therapeutic Condition of Muslims

Health is an issue associated closely with the social status. Accessibility to better health means a better or high social status. Better health is important for human existence also. As the health is affluence in human life hence regular health checkup is imperative for populace. Nevertheless, not all Muslim people check their health regularly owing to lack of awareness, poverty, and lack of time. Generally, Muslims test check out their health at the time when they are sick. Their health checkups and the venues are revealed in the following table.

Table 4.3

Health Checkup and the Venues in 2012

Health checkup	**Number**	**Percent**
Sub-Health post	58	12.44
Primary Health Center (P.H.C.)	22	4.72
Hospital	25	5.36
Traditional Healer	25	5.36
No response	336	72.10
Total respondents	**466**	**100.00**

Source: Field Survey, 2012

In the year 2012, only 105 Muslims have done regular checkup in modern health centers in the health posts, health centers and hospitals. 25

people took the help of traditional Muslim wizard healers. Among the respondents, 336 have no responses which mean no regular check up. People used to checkup their health when they get sick. It is deduced from this data that most people do not check their health regularly. They check their health only at the time of serious illness. Muslims are economically poor and they are hectic always in hard labor and lack health consciousness, therefore, they could not take care of their health in an apt way. Maximum people of Muslim settlement are agricultural laborers therefore; they always are engaged in work for fulfillment of their economic needs---that is *bread and butter*. Their economic source is mainly wage earning labor that requires hard work, even the over time work, therefore, they could not regularly do health checkup. They check their health only when they are only serious ill or when they are at the death bed. Only few people, only those few people who are somewhat economically balanced and health conscious, checked their health from time to time regularly. Those Muslims most affected by poor hygiene and poverty are women, and many still deliver babies at home in unsafe environments. Infants stand a high risk of infection due to unsanitary conditions. Most of the Muslim women are suffering from anemia because of giving birth to numerous children and also due to the strict Islamic credo of rejecting family planning. A case study of a Muslim woman clarifies the health stipulation.

Case Study Box 1

Safina Miya a Muslim Woman's Experience on Health

Safina Miya is a poor woman who has a poor economy and living a hard life. She is 30 years now. Her husband is engaged in wage earning labor work in the village. She has three children of 8 years, 6 years and 9 months respectively. The life is rigid and difficult for them. It is a challenge to arrange for bread and butter and to properly feed their family. As a housewife and a mother Safina is helpless, no one can give her and her family a salvation from this a state of affair because they are the victim of poverty. A part from this, they are illiterate and have a faith upon their conventional Islamic social norms, values embedded with superstitions of various sorts. They live in discomfort and have no alternative and time to think about how to feed the children and fulfill their basic needs in future related to individual and family health and education.

Owing to miserable economic condition, it is very hard for them to tackle the health related problems of their life. Safina is pregnant since five months. She knows just now about her pregnancy. The family will be adding one more new member in future. Now, she is not in a position to imagine now she will feed the baby to grow up as she has three young children still in the present to feed. The third one is still living on her breast-feeding and the fourth one is in her womb. She has no food on time and it is hard to get sufficient milk also. So, it is very hard for her to maintain her health and there exists probability that the baby to be born may be malnourished or may born with deformities or Safina as a mother may face health related maternity problems at the time of giving birth to the baby.

Safina is willing to do an abortion, but she cannot do it due to advice of doctor and that it was very late for the abortion. She is living in such a critical condition of mental impasse. At the same time, she cannot take the medical suggestion from an expert gynecologist related to her health and the health of the incoming baby because of acute poverty. As a mother, Safina is very worried about her lack of knowledge about pregnancy, menstrual cycle and postnatal problems she will be facing in future. Due to ignorance to family planning devices and illiteracy Safina and her family face the critical problem in daily lives. From this, it is clear that Muslims living here have the little knowledge and awareness about health and future activities, which depicts the poor social status of Muslims embedded with their low economic status.

Drinking Water Supply and Sanitation in Muslim settlement

Drinking Water Supply

Water is the lifeline of human being. Pure drinking water is indispensable for a hygienic life and supply of pure drinking water is necessary for all. In fact, water supply is the process of self-provision or provision by any parties to sources of water of different quality and quantity to different users. However, not all the people at all time are fortunate enough to have the provision of pure drinking water in least developed and developing countries. The sources of water determine the hygienic level of water. Using the water from river, brook, and ponds are not safe. In Muslim settlement sources of drinking water are varied.

Table 4.4

Sources of Drinking Water

Sources	Households	Percent
Tap	33	51.56
Spring	17	26.56
Pond	14	21.87
Total	64	100.00

Source: Field Survey, 2012

Here the majority households have used the water from tap followed by spring water, and rest of the households use local pond for drinking water. Nevertheless, in the faucet water is not available regularly therefore; sometimes they also depend upon spring water (*Mul ko pani*). In fact, tap water is available but the accessibility of water is not regular. It shows the underdevelopment scenario of the area not even having the regular supply of water in the Muslim settlement. A water tank has been constructed in the Muslim settlement with the help of District Development Office, Tanahun but the tank is always dry with no water at all. Hence, the majority of households have problems related to pure drinking water. Owing to economic reasons, Muslim people are not in a position to install their own private water tapes and the consequences are serious for example cases of gastrointestinal and numerous stomach problems. Children and elderly people are the worst victims.

Sanitation

Toilet is one of the most important needs of human life. However, majority people are not using toilet in Nepal because of lack of awareness, poverty, illiteracy and negligence. It is imperative that to analyze social-economic status, it is vital to outline the sanitation level of the people. In the Muslim settlements, the sanitations conditions are as follows.

Table 4.5

Types of Toilets

Toilet	Houses	Percent
Permanent	4	6.25
Temporary	23	35.93
No Toilet	37	57.81
Total	64	100.00

Source: Field survey, 2012

From the above table it is clear that the small number of permanent toilet is available in that area, whose number is only four. Large numbers of households have no any toilet and their number is 37. Moreover, temporary toilet is found in 23 households. We can define the data with an assertion that the large numbers of people are not using the modern toilet in Muslim settlement area owing to lack of health awareness, poverty and backwardness and this depicts the wretched condition of their social-economic status.

Pattern of Celebration of Festivals and Fairs

Analyzing various faiths and values of human society, two types of views seem unadulterated. These are ***Materialistic views** vs. **Spiritualism***. Materialistic views depend on what is seen from naked eyes or which is material whereas spiritualism believes in hereafter. Of these two worldviews, various beliefs and faiths have born, and Muslim religion and culture based on the philosophy of *Quran* is one of the popular religions worldwide.

According to Giddens (2001) variety of religion beliefs and organizations are so immense that scholars have found great difficulty in reaching a generally accepted definition of religion. In the west, most people identify religion with Christianity, the belief is a supreme being, who commands us to behave in a moral fashion on this earth and promise an afterlife to come. Yet, we certainly cannot define religion as a whole in these terms. These beliefs and many other aspects of Christianity are absent from most of the world's religions. The concept of religion is more related with emotion and sentiments of the people that drives people towards some benevolent doings. However, Marxist perspective alleges that, *religion is slow opium of masses* and the sign of fatalistic, suppressed and oppressed creatures. Nonetheless, it is incredibly imperative to trace the religious structure of an area to know about the level of development and progressive attitude of the people as claimed by Max Weber in *"Protestant Ethic and Spirit of Capitalism"*.

The religious structure of hill Muslims of Miyagaon is complex and diverse and with this complex structure, festivals and patterns of festivals and fairs celebration is affiliated. Festivals and fairs are observed for the satisfaction, social unity, solidarity as well as religious devotion. Muslim community in Miyagaon observes various fairs and festivals during the whole year. These are the main part of their culture and are as follows:

1. *New Year (Al-Hijara)*: Among the Muslims of Miyagaon, *Al-Hijara* is celebrated as the first day of the year according to the Islamic calendar. The first month is called *Muharram*. The first day of the starting year is also called *Ras-As-Sana* in which all the Muslims gather in the Mosque, starting the prayer and read Quran. They pray each other for peace and prosperity of their family and express the best wishes of the New Year among the community members by personal contact and phone. The hill Muslims of Miyagaon, Hukka observe fairs and festivals plainly by gathering and praying in the mosque.
2. ***Ashura***: It is observed on the tenth day of the first month of Muslim calendar i.e. *Muharram* by observing the *Roja* (fasting). This festival is celebrated in the memory of Martyr (the day of the death of the grand son of Hajrat Mohammad). Most of the hills Muslims of Miyagaon are from Sunni sect. Few Shia Muslims living in Miyagaon celebrate this festival somewhat differently by gathering and praying for progress and peace in the mosque.
3. ***The last Wednesday (Akhari Chahar Sambah*** Muslims observe this day in the memory of the relief of Hajarat Mohammed from illness. It is believed that the last Wednesday of the second month of the Islamic year is the holy day.
4. ***The birth day of Hajarat Muhammad (Miladunnabi)***: Muslims celebrate the birth day of Hajarat Muhammad called *Miladunnabi*. It is believed that Muhammad was born on the third month of the Islamic calendar. Some *Devbandi* (a new Muslim sect in Nepal) group Muslims who are somewhat close to Hindus, do not commemorate the birth day of Hajarat Muhammad (Miladunnabi).
5. ***The memory day of Abdul Kadir Jilani (the eleventh Sarif)***: The Muslims of Miyagaon commemorate the memory day of Abdul Kadir Jilani (the eleventh Sarif).
6. ***Muhammad's night visit to the heaven (Isra and Miraj)***: Once Muhammad visited Heaven from Mecca via Jerusalem. It was the holy visit, because of that Muslims honor and celebrates this visit as festival.

7. ***The yearly record night (Shab-E-Barat)***: This festival is celebrated on the 15th date of eighth month of the Islamic calendar. It is believed that Allah keeps the record of the birth, deaths and the continuation of life of certain men this day. Muslim folks of Miyagaon gather and do praying on this occasion.

8. ***Praying for deceased members***: The family members visit the courtyards at night to remember, honor and get blessing from Allah for their deceased members. In Hukka the Muslim people do these activities residing at their home and visiting the courtyards. On this occasion, they prepare diverse food items and feed to their relatives and poor people. Before taking the food people do fasting in the name of Allah.

9. ***The arrival night of Quran (Layalat Al-Qadr):*** This occasion is called the night of command or the night of consultation. It is believed to be the day of holy Quran coming down to the earth; it means Allah provides his direction through Quran. The Muslims of Miyagaon call this night *the night of power*-the power of holy Quran that enlightens the people. They believe that the sanctimonious words of Quran came to existence in this holy night. This festival is important for religious purpose rather than enjoying.

10. ***The ending of fasting (Eid Ul Fitra)***: At the end of Ramadan, *Eid Ul Fitra* is celebrated in Muslim community. It is observed according to the Muslim calendar. In Arabian language, the meaning of *Eid* is festival and the word of *Fitra* is the ending of *Brat* (Fasting). Charity or gift is also important on this occasion. At the last month of the Ramadan the moon is viewed, i.e. *Eid ka Chand* during which sometimes conflicts occurs on the issue of catching a glimpse of the moon. The important function is the collective praying at the open field. After praying, all the participants exchange best wishes and congratulate each other.

11. ***The occasion of sacrifice (Eid Ul Adha)***: On this occasion, Muslims sacrifice the goats, and buffalos. In other countries cows are also slaughtered but not in Hukka due to national legal system of Nepal that regards cow as a national animal and prohibits cow slaughter. In this way, all the process of the festivals and fairs endures in the

name of *Allah*-the almighty.

In Hukka as the majority of people are living with a common poor status *hence* they celebrate and observe their festival only for religious gratifications in a simple form only for the pleasure of their own and children and hence giving a continuation to their religion. They celebrate their festival however the celebration status is according to their condition. Few household celebrate their festival in pomp *and show* (ostentatious) way by borrowing money from others-especially from the rich peoples and relatives. The Muslims festivals and fairs observation pattern in the hills of Miyagaon, Hukka is different from the rest of the world owing to close cultural contacts with the non-Muslims for centuries and also due to various economic and political reasons. The Muslims are not allowed to slaughter cow during their festivals/fairs and are also not allowed to propagate Islam openly. Observation patterns of festivals and many of the Islamic traditions have changed in Miyagaon in the course of time and also due to the influence of dominant Hindu religion of the Hindu neighbors.

Gender Stipulation in Household Decision-making in Muslim Settlement

Most of the gender social norms in Hukka have a murky facet, which constitutes a significant source of disparities between men and women in the society. Here, social norms usually constitute not just a difference but an inequality based on religious perpetuated disparities of various sorts in day-to-day life. They have been permeating virtually every sphere of activity: they define what tasks men and women should perform how they should interact in public, how women should behave and dress in public and private. There is also a difference in their access to private property and to income-earning opportunities. Because of strong patriarchal traditions, Muslim women neither own nor directly control any property. Lack of education and owing to other social-economic reasons they also have lesser access than men to jobs and other sources of income except wage earning labor work in agricultural sector and small business. Given women's primary responsibility for household chores, this becomes a particular constraint.

Women in big households or in female-headed households (which are more susceptible to poverty) are placed at an obvious disadvantage. Nevertheless, even in male-headed households, although women are claiming some advantage from the families' endowments in fulfilling their responsibilities, there is no guarantee of access to male-controlled income. In broad-spectrum, gender disparities in access to private property and labor, income are creating gender differences, women's increasing dependence on males in varying degrees in Muslim settlement in Miyagaon, Hukka consequently resulting in the sharp corrosion of social-economic status of women. The table illustrates the prevailing gender situation in Muslim households.

Table 4.6

Gender Stipulation in Household Decision-making

Number of Households	Decision Making role of women	Frequency	%
64	No role	8	12.5
	Partial role	11	17.18
	Advisory role	35	54.68
	Absolute role	10	15.62
	Total	64	100.00

Source: Field Survey, 2012

Of the total 64 households; eight household heads (both husband and wife) claimed that there is no role of women in household decision-making. Only eleven have partial role, thirty-five have advisory role and rest of the ten have absolute role. Advisory role of women is common which lacks vigorous chipping in of women. Here the vital decisions related to money matters and all crucial issues are dealt by senior males of the family. The Islamic traditional norms, customs and values are responsible for creating disparities. Out of household decision-making, disparity in wage labor earning is the most acute in creating disparities. Most of the households claimed of this sort of discrimination in work places. Here labor disparity in the cases of Muslim women, has been looked at from two angles in terms of hours of daily work undertaken by men and women, and a source of difference in interest. The more stiff the division of labor, the more the conflict of interest between male and female.

Since for strong patriarchal tradition and patriarchic norms, women's working hours is longer than men (usually women work 5-6 hours more than men) and there is a fairly rigid division of domestic task responsibility and chores. Women, for instance, are largely responsible for cooking food, for gathering fuel, agricultural works, children rearing and men for wage earning and public activities. Many women are involved in wage earning labor work and agricultural works along with males but they are bound to do household works also thus they face the dichotomy of dual role – *household chore vs. agricultural works/wage earning labor works.* This dichotomy is creating hindrances in women's social-economic enhancement. For the fulfillment of daily economic needs, a persistent pressure is created on women consequently increasing their dependence on males. At the same time those women who are engaged in wage earning are not getting the proper wages, it means they are facing discriminations in salary with two different wages for the same work and women are getting less wages than man is, even for the same work.

The yoke of patriarchal discriminations are so sharp in Miyagaon, Hukka that usually every praying time (Friday) when Muslim man gather in Mosque they used to gossip on current issues on social, political, issues of women and household affairs. Women of good character are supposed to avoid from attending such gathering of males. Muslim community has internalized these social norms that is restricting woman rights and mobility. Tendency exists in the cases of restricting the free movement of Muslim womenfolk during their menstrual period same to that of Hindu upper caste women. These hierarchy and norms marks family behavior also that tends to explain community interactions and are important hindrances fading female social-economic status.

Male sensation and their perceptions about women's appropriate roles and abilities serve as an additional source of disparity. Women are usually perceived as being less capable than men are, or their participation in public is considered inappropriate or unnecessary. Nevertheless, interestingly, few Muslim female members responded that they are getting some support from their spouse and other male members of family. They claimed that it would have been difficult to be involved in wage earning activities if their husband and other male members (sons) and other senior male relatives would have denied permission to them. Women members also claimed that their husband in some cases had helped them even in performing their household chores so that their wives can go and work for wage earning activities or involve in any sort of public work. They however reported that there are numerous social-cultural and gender related issues (e.g. male bigotry) and discriminations that are deteriorating the social-economic status of Muslim female. Muslim women are even debarred from praying in the mosque.

Economic Status

Economic structure is intimately interrelated to occupational structure and livelihood. In fact, the occupation determines the economic structure. The economic status is also embedded with social status of the people. One of the important considerations of economic indictors is the scope of the income sources the people consider when determining the "household income". Income received from jobs, and other sources are imperative. Income sources and alimony might be spontaneously considered in a calculation of household income and for the evaluation of economic status. Embedded to economic structure, household income also includes income earned from the "informal economy" (e.g., jobs that pay cash but have no benefits or job security) particularly in communities of recent immigrants, squatters and minorities. These income sources may be ones that respondents do not wish to disclose or for which they would have difficulty determining a monetary value.

In broad-spectrum, the outline of the economic status of Muslims is as follows:

Occupational Structure of Households

There are several areas where Marxism has been analyzed from sociological and anthropological perspectives. A good deal of effort has been expanded in an attempt to adapt the basic idea of a necessary conflict between labor and capital to the conditions of contemporary societies. All these efforts have taken the form of new theories of social class to take account of changes in the patterns of property ownerships changes in relationships at work, class divisions, and rise of elitism and side-by-side growth of more conscious middle class also, exploitation, growing unrests and the reasons behind conflicts also hang about of the essence. It has been lengthily comprehended in Nepal that it is practically unfeasible to comprehend and solve the problems related to social unrests in the absence of a proper mechanism explaining the affiliation between the growing elitism with its historical legacy and the scramble for livelihood, social/cultural, economic and political rights on the part of underprivileged people at the present.

Affiliated to economic structure, occupation is a set of activities centered on an economic role and usually associated with earning a living-for example, a trade or profession. An occupation is a social role that is determined by the general division of labor within a society. As a specialization of an individual's function in society, occupation is an important factor defining a person's prestige, class position, and style of life (Dictionary of Sociology, 1999). Occupation is also an important part and facet of living human life. Occupation illustrates the position of people. Muslims of Miyagaon, Hukka are involved in various types of occupation. The table depicts the numbers of Muslims respondents engaged in different occupations and their percentage.

Table 4.7

Occupational Status of Respondents

Occupation	Number
Agricultural sector	46
Government service (job)	1
Business	5
Labourhood	4
Foreign service	38
Teaching field	6
Total Employed	100

Source: Field Survey, 2012

The occupations of Muslim of Miyagaon vary. They have different occupations. Of the all total 64 households there are 100 economically active population engaged in different occupations. There are many people from the same family who are having jobs. Nevertheless, the large numbers of respondents are engaged in agricultural sector. There are 46 respondents engaged in agricultural sector. Womenfolk's do their housework chores and takes care of their children. The second largest occupational populaces are Foreign Service holder, they are 38 in number. Moreover, other adult Muslims are engaged in government sector jobs, business, and labour works and in teaching field. Their numbers stood at one, five, four, six, respectively. Moreover, rest of the Muslims has no any job because they are either students or agricultural land owners renting land to tenants. This data reveals that people with high profile occupation is very exceptional among the Muslims of Hukka. Poor illiterate people do not have access to good occupation.

Most of the poor people in Nepal live in rural areas yet still a huge percentage of poor people struggle in cities trying to make ends meet. Similar to national trend, most Muslim youths leave for cities to help their parents financially. Many youths go overseas for employment opportunities in gulf countries, Malaysia etc while others study in cities and/or work there. Kids beyond their school time, spend most of their daily life doing house-hold works. The impact of a decade long civil war waged by Maoist insurgents has left behind its impact in Miyagaon. It has been reported by respondents that during the insurgency period (1996-2006) this village was as empty as ghost village. With the end of insurgency in 2006 peace has returned but people are deprived due to lack of modern techniques to manage the available resources, low-productivity land, roads to obtain agriculture inputs and to sell agriculture produce. Many of the social indicators in Miyagaon are the lowest compared to other villages of Nepal. Consequently, people's economic condition is low and fragile throughout the year keeping them *in their hand to mouth* all the time. Economy in Miyagaon, Hukka has taken the form of distinguishing different capital fractions and of providing an account of the monopoly phase of elites—both Muslims and Hindus. How differences in social-economic status develop when elitism is institutionalized and sharing of productive resources to commoners is the issue of special enquiry. The growing but latent unrest, scramble for controlling resources on the part of Muslim masses but the failure to upgrade the status, conflict of interest between dominant and subordinate segments in the system, the legitimacy of the existing pattern of distribution of scarce resources may create future tensions. If there is the greater questioning of the validity of the distribution of political power, political actions and scarce resources, the more likely the common Muslims to be at odds against the prevailing system. Likewise, when greater is the ideological merger of members of subordinate segments, the additional the chances of polarization of subjugated segments of the society. Given this veracity, hence, the need of the time is to ponder on the grievances of underprivileged Muslim sections of the society by having a consideration of their bleak social-economic tribulations.

Monthly Household Income

The monthly household income is that income which is the total income of people within a month. Income of people is of different range in different people or households. People do works and earn livings. Some people earn more and some earn fewer but majority people do works for their survival. A continuous income is necessary for the survival and the well-being of the individual as well as the family. Particularly skilled people have high chances of earning more than unskilled people who have fewer chances of earning more money and in making high living standards. The monthly household incomes of Muslims are given in the table.

Table 4.8

Monthly Household Average Income

Income in Nepali Rupees (per month)	Households	Percent (%)
Below 2000	15	23.43
2000-4000	12	18.75
4000-8000	5	7.81
8000- Above	32	50.00
Total	64	100.00

Source: Field Survey, 2012

15 households economic condition is squat. They have their monthly income lower than Nepali Rupees 2000 (It is to be noted that one Us dollar is equivalent to 98 Nepali rupees). 12 households are earning two to four thousand rupees per month, five households have four to eight thousand and 32 have more than eight thousand earnings per month. From these data, it is clear that only 32 people earned more than 8000 and maximum people do not earn adequate money to feed their family and are in penury. Some people have gone to foreign country therefore their income is high but maximum people are living below the deficiency stripe in this area. Therefore, as a whole from the national perspective a number of low-income people are living in Muslim settlement but out of a population of 64 households, 32 families have a monthly income 8000 and above which shows comparatively the sound economic status. On the other hand, maximum people do agricultural works in the study area having abundant landholdings. Male and female of the family does work but the agricultural output is low despite hard labor consequently their life style is low and wretched. The cultural concept, *culture of poverty* and strict Islamic religious credo is creating a dilemma of *poverty amidst plenty* of land and income. They cannot manage their available resources properly, fail to fulfill their

basic needs easily and cannot escape from fatalism and *culture of poverty* cycle. They have land but agro-production is insufficient to feed because agriculture is subsistence. They rely upon their income but income is unable to enhance their social-economic status consequently their social-economic status is low. The failure to manage available resources properly is proving to be a momentous problem.

Land Holdings of Muslims

Landholding is possession of property in the form of land: a complete landholding. People have different landholding status. Some people have more land, some people have less quantity of land, and some are landless. Landless people are also known as squatters or *Sukumbasi* in Nepali. The acquisition of land by land hungry people is extensive in Nepal. The table makes it more lucid.

Table 4.9

Household Landholdings (Dry Land)

Household Landholdings Dry land (in acres)	Number of Households	Percent (%)
Below 3	25	39.6
4 to 8	23	35.9
9 to 15	10	15.6
16 to 23	6	9.0
Total	64	100.00

Source: Field Survey, 2012

Different types of landholdings prevail in Hukka. Dry land is meant mainly for cash crops. The number of households with dry land landholdings below 3 acres of land is 25 in number making a percentage of 39.6. Likewise, only 6 households are having the highest acres of dry land landholding ranging from 16 to 23 acres. These 6 households are the exclusive elite Muslim groups of Miyagaon, Hukka. This data clarifies that no Muslim is a landless squatter which depicts a feudal tendency of occupying more and more land that prevails among the Muslim masses. It is also a stipulation of plenty of resources controlled by Muslim masses but living in penury owing to the failure to utilize the resources properly.

Table 4.10

Household Landholdings (Paddy Land)

Household landholdings Paddy Land (in acres)	Number of Households	Percent (%)
1 to 2	25	39.0
3 to 4	9	14.6
5 to 10	4	6.2
No Land	26	40.20
Total	64	100.00

Source: Field Survey, 2012

Muslim people have different types of landholding position. Houses are made in small piece of land with very limited area and huge chunk of free land are maintained close or at a distance to houses. 25 households have less than 1-2 acres of land for paddy cultivation. 9 household's have 3 to 4 acres of paddy land. The majority of households-- 26 households have no paddy land hence they are deficient in rice production the main staple food of the Muslims. Nevertheless, out of 64 households, only 38 households have paddy land. Most of the Muslim people have the attitude to take up more and more land-a long-established feudal Nepali notion. According to this, the social prestige is linked with land. Almost all have the attitude to hold more land—a feudalistic Nepali perception embedded with social and cultural realities owing to the state's inability to deliver services and help to its citizens. Although some households have sufficient landholdings nevertheless their living conditions has not improved despite hard work, rather deteriorated, an example of *poverty amid plenty*. Likewise, many of the Muslim youths are working in Middle East (gulf countries), they are sending remittances, but the social, cultural, educational, health, sanitation and overall living condition of their family members has not improved under the vicious cycle of *culture of poverty*. For instance even many households are lacking toilets in their houses owing to lack of awareness. Muslim households are not in a position to appropriately utilize their available resources—an example of *poverty amid plenty*. The remittances earned from foreign jobs have been wasted in unproductive sectors, invested more on affording agricultural land or house construction or on children education.

Attire Use Pattern of Muslims

Attires or clothing is a part of basic needs of human being. Clothing also represents the economic status of a family. The value of dress of Muslim community in Miyagaon is guided by the norms of Quran. It should be loose, simple; the dress should cover the whole body, artistic, suitable for gender identity, and warm etc. The color is not fixed for women but white dress is fixed for males. Attires are equal and situations are different. Some of them cannot buy attires or clothes for them and their children. However, all the people try to get the things of eating, wearing, and lodging for their happiness and maintenance. The study of wearing clothes denotes the economic status of Muslims. Therefore, it is important to study the costumes used by them. Like other community people, they receive clothes from their rich relatives or from the relatives working abroad and some buy themselves during the festivals and special occasions during the festivals and special occasions. The Muslim people of Hukka wear the dresses like other people (Hindus and Buddhists) of that locality which is because of the impact of Sanskritization on Muslim lifestyle. The dressing pattern is similar to Aryan Brahman, Chhetri and ethnic Magar people. The males used to wear pant, shirt, trouser (*paijama*), Nepali cap (called *Dhaka topi*), waistcoat, loose shirt (*kurta*), coat etc. The females wear Sari, blouse (called *choli* in Nepali), kurta, lower garment (*lungi*), skirt and ornaments according to their income and status. Wearing the veil (*Burka*) is the traditional culture of women in Muslim community. However, due to sanskritization with mainstream Hindu society, in the field observation no single Muslim women was found wearing the veil or *Burka* (*purdah*).This is beyond the customary system of Muslims. This is a unique change in hill Muslims custom. It is positive sign in the path of the empowerment of Muslim women.

Accommodation (Housing)

Housing Style and Types of Houses

The size of house and rooms depicts the economic structure of a family. The study of number of rooms in house makes comprehensible the social-economic condition of the Muslim people. Therefore, the study of household condition is imperative in research. In the Muslim settlement in Hukka, the houses are small and rooms are less spacious. The conditions of houses of the settlement have been presented in table.

Table 4.11

Types of Houses

Types	Households	Percent
Permanent	43	67.18
Temporary	21	32.81
Total	64	100.00

Source: Field Survey, 2012

The numbers of permanent houses called *Pakki Ghar* are 43 in the settlement area. The *Pakki Ghar* in rural part is one with tin roofs and stone walls. Whereas, temporary house called *Kacchi Ghar* is made with thatch and mud used mainly by poor people. The number of temporary households or *Kacchi Ghar* is 21 having only the limited number of rooms. The permanent house has five or six rooms and temporary has two or three rooms. The population density is high hence the accommodation is congested and the life is hard and tough. There exists the problem of proper ventilation in temporary houses, which are always crowded. This is creating an adverse effect on the health mainly of the children, women and old people. Housing condition depicts the low economic status of the Muslims.

Commodities/Physical facilities at Home

People want to entertain in their life but not every house has the availability for all things of entertainment. The nature of people is such that they wish for to entertain and do recreation in their life. Some Muslim houses have some entertainment commodities as depicted.

Table 4.12

Commodities of Entertainment

Commodities	Number of Sets	Responses Percent
Radio	35	7.51
TV	3	0.64
Solar1	8	3.86
Cupboard	18	3.86
Motorbike	1	0.21
Mobile telephone	23	4.93
Have no commodity	368	78.96
Total	466	100.00

Source: Field Survey, 2012

From the above table it is clear that out of total 64 households, 35 households are using radio. Black/White Television is available in three households. This region lacks electrification hence solar panels for generating electricity are used in 18 households. Only the single person is using motorbike. Mobile telephone facilities have been used by 23 households. The radio and television are the prime medium for entertainment. All houses have no availability of all entertainment things. Likewise, many houses lack commodities of entertainments owing to the verity of economic condition. Not all people can buy and use things of expensive entertainment in their house. Only radio seems more popular in this part of the country which is a major electronic source. No one is using computer and internet is this settlement which is a gloomy situation in this 21st century. The world of telecommunication and information technology is far from their life. As economically diverse status people are living in Muslim settlement in Miyagaon, Hukka, many of the economically sound people may be in a position to think about affording computer and hiring internet facilities in future. As many of their relatives are working as laborers in gulf countries, internet, Skype may be quite practical to them to communicate with each other.

5

REPURCUSSIONS OF POVERY VS PLENTY DICHOTOMIES

Nepal is a rich country from the perspective of the availability of natural resources but the country is inhabited by economically poor people who are unable to harness the available resources properly. The country is prosperous from biodiversity and social-cultural point of view. Nevertheless, it is primarily a semi-feudal agrarian country. Majority of people live in rural areas and rely on agriculture. Indeed poor as indicated by indicators of development, the World Bank has categorized Nepal as one of the poor countries of the world since the publication of the World Development Reports in the early eighties. Although the modern development indicators show that Nepal is one of the poorest countries in the world, it is appallingly rich in bio-diversity and socio-cultural diversities. Bio-diversity and indigenous nationalities are indeed very much interconnected and socio-cultural diversity is characterized by diversity in caste, ethnicity, language, religion, culture and region.

Despite diversities, in Nepal, the size of various ethnic/caste groups in the total population was hardly known before 1990 despite Nepal being a multiethnic, multilingual and multicultural country. The eleventh census of 2011, for the first time, identified more than 125 ethnic/caste groups and more than 123 languages in multiethnic Nepal. A long history of the continuation of political autocracy, social exclusion, marginalization and exclusion from access to resources, services and opportunities, disempowerment, cultural and ritual debasement, discrimination and marginalization (on the basis of religious affiliation, caste, ethnicity, culture, language, territorial/geographical origin/remoteness and gender, and capacity constraints) are the major impediments for the inclusion of diverse ethnic and caste groups in the national development efforts. Most of the achievements and resources through the past development process has gone to governing caste and ethnic groups, however, the issues of ethnicity and religion in Nepal is exclusive and dissimilar from other countries. The diffident subordinate groups which came to be created slowly in Nepal were not due to colonialism or voluntary or involuntary migration or annexation but were created slowly by internal processes in the majority of cases. However, census reports and studies conducted by the Nepalese and international scholars give picture of multifarious social structure as well as counting numbers of caste/ethnicity, language and religion.

Hill Muslims called *Churoute* living in hills of Kihun VDC of Tanahun district possess their distinct socio-cultural and economic features and are involved in commercial or industrial undertakings, but the majority of them are either unskilled laborers or small-scale subsistence farmers, with no lower-level government civil servants even. These hill Muslims speak their own *Miya* language which is different from Nepali but little bit similar to Hindi language. However, they can speak good Nepali also. Ignorance and backwardness are rampant among hill Muslims, and this has led to their forfeiture of their human rights in the country. Even in the faith that they profess, their knowledge of Islamic principles and culture is very meager, and they do need guidance and direction in this respect. Many of them are Muslims in name only, but hardly know anything else about Islam. There are high chances that their emotions may be easily manipulated maliciously by Islamic radicals in future. The main reason behind this is the lack of awareness and backwardness of common Muslims in educational field.

The religious schools (*madrassas*) are unable to produce the skilled personnel and professionals that could match the students demand as well as market demand. Consequently, the products of such *madrassas* are unable to get any job in the government sectors and hence they are compelled to do jobs in the *maktab* (small madrassas), Mosque as Imam (one who leads the prayer), *Muazzin* (one who calls the people for the prayer by reciting chants of Quran *azan*) where they get a meager salary per month. Hence, how it is possible to uplift the life style and the educational standard? Moreover, Nepali Government has not ever given due consideration to bring the Muslims in the mainstream. It does not fully support the *madrassas* financially and morally which can play a role to educate the Muslim people and help the nation to reach a respectable literacy rate by the inclusion of the Muslims in the mainstream. Moreover, it has been found that the government authorities are creating several problems during the registration and issuance of citizen certificates and other documents. Even they are positively interfering with the curriculums taught in *madrassas*. An example is that in *madrassas* beyond Islamic education, modern subjects have been introduced recently as Nepali, English, Science, and Mathematics which are quite similar to the national curriculum. Many of the Muslims are expressing their dissatisfactions towards this initiation. They allege that modern education is of no use to them. But on the other hand, the positive implications of modern western education may be that it may create an environment to slow down the rise of Islamic fundamentalism emerging from madrassas.

There are other reasons for the dissatisfaction of Muslims. The Muslims has been deprived of the right to practice Islamic personal law, because there are no such laws in the country, though Islam dawned on it in the fifth century of the *Hijri* calendar, according to existing historical records. They have to follow the non-Islamic rules regarding marriage, divorce, sacrificing animal in the name of Allah during the occasion of *Eidul Azhah* and others. Muslims face troubles while following their religious traditions in many different spheres. They follow the non-Islamic rules regarding marital break up, nuptials, sacrificing animal (sacrificing cow is restricted in predominantly Hindu dominated country). But with the country declared a secular state in 2006, the religious minorities of Nepal have got a new recognition with national holidays declared on festivals like *Eid* and Christmas. However still, the issues of religious minorities don't seem to hold a prominent place, unlike the much-vaunted indigenous and *ethnicities* issues and their rights. Contrary to the so-called violent world image of Muslims generated by westerners' Muslim phobia, hill Muslims of Miyagaon Kihun are a quiet and peace-loving community. So far there have been no religious tensions in this village. The religious harmony and communal solidarity has been well maintained in the society.

In a society with mass unemployment, majority of youths are opting to go for foreign employment, especially to the Gulf countries, hence there is an acute shortage of labor power in the village. Another good percentage of the population is in agriculture and local business. There is only one Muslim male who has joined government service. If we leave aside few school teachers teaching at primary level in local schools there is not even a single person in security services, e.g. who has joined the Nepal Army and the Police. However, some Muslims are quite active in local politics. Despite no state support in development works Muslims of Miyagaon don't seem to grumble much, though they would be glad if the government provided them even a minimum support. The community believes largely in themselves than to wait for state support to come. This can be proven by the initiative of a group of men who, while working in the Gulf, send back money collectively to the village in order to help in their cause.

Besides, there is something special about the community that other groups can also follow: People in Miyagaon help each other in times of difficulty. Especially, they pool money to celebrate festivals like *Eid*, when the rich help the poor in the celebrations. Though the poor status of women's empowerment is an overall scenario of the whole country, Muslim women's participation in politics and decision-making in Miyagaon Kihun is comparatively lesser than the other communities. Nevertheless, it seems the winds of change are slowly being felt even in Miyagaon, Kihun. The women have founded their *women group*, carrying the vision of working for women's empowerment and fighting against polygamy, suppression and many other gender related social evils. Similarly, the youths have formed a youth club, Islamic Youth Society, which often organizes sports and other social and cultural events.

The Muslims of Miyagaon of Kihun are quite similar to hill dweller Hindus in terms of language, appearance, and costumes. Their culture is very much mixed with hilly *(Pahadi)* ambience. Over time, they adopted typical hilly *(Pahadi)* norms in clothes, language and cultural patterns, though not leaving their religious customs. Interestingly, it is common to see Muslim men going around in typical Nepali dress called (*daura suruwal*) and Nepali cap (*Dhaka topi)* ensemble, some of them can even be seen coming for prayer (*Namaaz*) clad in such attires. This shows a close affinity between hill Muslim culture and the culture of hill dweller Hindus. Despite these cultural empathy, hill Muslims of Miyagaon, Kihun, are facing diverse sorts of social-economic tribulations owing to various sorts of socio-cultural and economic restrictions and exclusions. They are not capable of combating their backwardness in social, economic, and political matters, nor are they capable of confronting religious discriminations and implications. Youths prefer foreign job in gulf countries due to social exclusion and also because of the lack of local job opportunities. However, Muslims living here have the great desire to serve the nation in all respects so their reorganization and the establishment of general religious rights and social inclusion will create more devotion towards the nation and they may be able to contribute in a better way.

Based on these aforesaid discussions this chapter aligns to repercussions (consequences) of dichotomies of *Poverty vs. Plenty* scenario embedded with social-economic status, social exclusion and consequent tribulations the Muslims are facing at the present owing to their prevailing social-economic status, social discriminations and social exclusion. The *economic* dimension of Muslims relates to the use and insinuation of income, available resources, the competitiveness and the future viability of Muslims family economy and the woe. Inefficient economic structures, inappropriate expertise as well as the diversity of income sources for households are important elements of Muslims' social and economic status.

The *social* dimension relates to questions of opportunities and access to social amenities and services compared to other economic indicators. The issues of equal opportunities and society's ethical standard of behavior can also be considered as embedded to the social dimension. Side by side the Muslims' history as migrants and their religious minded nature are also the veracities influencing the social and economic status of Muslims. It is an authenticity that Muslims of this region migrated from other neighboring regions like Rampur of Palpa and Lamjung districts also due to social discrimination and *social exclusion* in their native land. Rampur Valley of Palpa district is located some 70 km east from Tansen, the district headquarters of Palpa. Rampur is the largest Muslim settlement in Palpa, with approximately 70 households and 700 people. The other larger Muslim settlements in the Hills are in this Miyagaon, Hukka of Kihun VDC (with 64 Muslim households) of Tanahun district. It is with the Muslims of Rampur that the Muslims of Miyagaon, Kihun are maintaining socio-cultural, economic, and marital and relationships of many other sorts.

In Hukka, Kihun village, the Muslims migrated over the period of time, thus making a settlement of Miyagaon. Behind the reasons of some Muslims migration to Kihun, the socio-cultural and economic hardness is one of the causes, others being aspiration for better business opportunities, acquisition of cheap agricultural land in the hills of Kihun. However, they are bound to face diverse sorts of socio-cultural, legal, political and many other economic complications. In addition, it is the ramifications of social-economic status that is creating diverse sorts of snag.

Repercussion of Social-economic Status and Tribulations

Embedded with social-economic status *poverty* is the key issue. It is the deficiency of fundamental human needs, such as clean water, nutrition, health care, education, clothing and shelter, because of the inability to afford them. This is also referred to as absolute poverty or **destitution**. Relative poverty is the condition of having fewer resources or less income than others within a society or country, or compared to worldwide averages. Poverty reduction in many countries has historically been a result of economic growth as increased levels of production, such as modern industrial technology, made more wealth available for those who were otherwise too poor to afford them. Investments in modernizing the agriculture and increasing yields is considered the core of the antipoverty effort, given that the major quarters of the poor are rural farmers. Economic encouragement includes extending property rights, especially to land, to the poor, and making financial services, notably savings, accessible. Inefficient institutions, corruption and political instability can also discourage investment. Aid and government support in health, education and infrastructure helps growth by increasing human and physical capital but it is not the situation in Miyagaon, Hukka.

Noble Laureate Amartya Sen (1998) has said that to tackle poverty it is vital to meet nutritional requirements, to escape avoidable disease, to be sheltered, to be clothed, to be able to travel, and to be educated. However, in Miyagaon, Hukka the situation of poverty prevails under the plenty of resources (natural, human and economic) characterized by severe deprivation of fundamental awareness, basic human needs, including food, safe drinking water, sanitation facilities, health, shelter, education and information. Not the income but access to services and the failure to manage the available resources properly are the grave tribulations. It also includes a lack of productive resources to ensure sustainable livelihoods; malnutrition; ill health; limited or lack of access to education and other basic services; increased morbidity and mortality from illness; inadequate housing; unsafe environments and religious discrimination and social exclusion. It is also characterized by lack of participation in decision making and in civil, social and cultural life. It occurs in many countries as mass poverty in many developing countries, pockets of poverty amid wealth in developed countries, loss of livelihoods as a result of economic recession, sudden poverty as a result of disaster or conflict, the poverty of low-wage workers, and the utter destitution of people who fall outside family support systems, social institutions and safety nets.

Muslim people in Miyagaon, Hukka are victims of living with paucity and mismanaged resources (material, cultural and social), are the subject to derisory that preclude them from having a standard of living which is regarded as acceptable by broader society generally. As a result they are excluded and marginalized from participating in activities which are considered the norm for other people in mainstream society. Their backwardness is greatly affecting the development of the social, economic, as well as cultural structures of the population. It is the consequences of the vicious cycles of backwardness and poverty embedded with *culture of poverty* that Muslims are experiencing here. Muslim settlement is a swarming area where houses are joined together in a cluster with a low level of living standard and accommodation which in turn is creating various complications for them. There are problems created among Muslims owing to flimsy social and economic status like the degrading land resources, depletion of available natural resources, youth migration for foreign jobs, labour shortage, backwardness, ignorance and poverty etc. Other concerns include the Muslims' psychology of feeling insecure surrounded by majority Hindus. The nature and attitudes vary greatly among Muslims in this settlement. Feeling of insecurity can prepare a fertile ground for rise of religious fundamentalism that can create long term effect on the security of the whole South-Asia.

Most of the Muslim people do possess plenty of land, however their houses are crowded and they are living in congested area which is due to the mismanagement of land resources and also fragile economic conditions. In contrast to these problems, maximum number of children use to go to school for study because educational institution is accessible in their locality. However, owing to delicate social and economic status, parents are less aware towards children's education and are unaware towards the insinuation of education. Social condition of the area is not cheering and economic condition is squat but as some people have gone for foreign jobs hence some household's economic condition is healthier than others. Majority of people do subsistence agriculture work with less income consequently, their economic status is stumpy. It is comprehensible that the overall condition of the Muslims is fragile which is creating direct implications on their living standard which is in turn is creating various sorts of tribulations and consequences. In fact, upshot of being a *religious alien* and implications on social-economic status has added to their tribulations, which are as follows.

Tribulations of the Muslims

Families become apathetic and indifferent towards broader society due to numerous reasons. In the process of socio-cultural-economic and political augmentation, the family has to confront with an assortment of problems. In the Muslim settlement, due to the limited adoption of modern agricultural technologies such as nitrogen fertilizers, pesticides and new irrigation methods the agricultural production has not increased to the extent of eliminating poverty. However, mass use of Chinese goods has made what were once considered luxuries, such as mobiles, radio and television sets inexpensive and thus accessible to many who were otherwise poor to afford them. However, rises in the costs of living is making poor people less able to afford items. Poor Muslims having insufficient food production are unable to spend a greater portion of their budgets on food than richer people. As a result, poor households and those near the poverty threshold are particularly vulnerable to food prices hike.

There are scores of consequences behind the backwardness and marginalization of the Muslims. Lack of infrastructures of development is creating the problem, lack of electricity supply in Miyagaon settlement; education and healthcare not reaching the poor Muslims are the common phenomenon. Due to lack of occupation, unemployed Muslims are forced to migrate to large cities and foreign countries for temporary work. For those unable to find jobs (local or abroad) the consequences they are facing is the vicious cycle of poverty. Poor health and education, however, is severely affecting the productivity at work. Inadequate nutrition in childhood is undermining the ability of individuals to develop their full physical mental capabilities. Deficiency of indispensable minerals such as iodine and iron for children is hindering physical growth and mental development which can seriously hamper the future generation which will consequently exacerbate the process of backwardness, proletariatisation and the impoverishment process of the Muslim masses.

Beyond these, there are other tribulations too of Muslims. Major tribulations of Muslims of Miyagaon settlement embedded with their social-economic status are as follows:

Social Tribulations

A social predicament is a condition that at least some people in a community views it as being undesirable. Everyone would agree about some social problems, such as unemployment, poverty, murders and robbery or drug addiction etc. Other social problems may be viewed as such by certain groups of people (Giddens, 2000). In broad-spectrum, social tribulations are multifaceted and create hardships for all and the society as a whole. The prevailing social-economic scenario of backwardness is creating multifaceted problems. It means that the genesis of social tribulations is in the prevailing social-economic status of the Muslims that has its genesis in social exclusion, the family, social structure and conservative Islamic religious credo.

Among the Muslims, family sizes diverge sharply. It is apparent from the previous chapter that majority households have large family structure. Even households having seven members are common. Five member households are also common in Muslim settlements. Muslim religious sacrament of regarding family planning as unethical and unholy has prepared the ground that no any male or female member of this Muslim settlement was found to have opted to family planning techniques. They are even reluctant to talk on family planning. This is the major reason behind the big family structure of households. Nevertheless, despite large family structure, it is a veracity that Muslims' houses are very small and maximum numbers of houses have only one room. By the distribution of family members, the size of house is very small. Single room serves as kitchen, bedroom and store. Consequently, their way of life is stiff. Low quality housing and the brittle life-chances conditions are the repercussion of fragile social status. Muslim families are huge but most of these children are lacking excellence in education and many go to religious school (*Madrassas*) owing to various reasons. In addition, children are obligated to slot in different forms of domestic labor and other vulnerable works bearing high risks.

Muslims are having their landholding but their economic status is totally dependant upon their hardworking, agriculture, wage earning income, small business. Their traditional occupation of making and selling bangles has vanished. Muslims are unable to elevate their status easily, they are becoming *isolated* day by day from the broader society, and a condition of *pauperization* is emerging hence preparing a ground for the conversion of these Muslims into waged people (*proletariat*) under a fast process of *proletariatisation*. Under a ferocious thrash about for upgrading social-economic status but with little achievement, the Muslim apathy in national issues seems trifling. The inhabitants of Muslims settlements have emerged in the historical context and have adjusted themselves to the new environment. Nevertheless, marginalization, backwardness, illiteracy, poverty, religious fundamentalism etc are tribulations of Muslims settlement with the ugly blemishes of religious discriminations of being the religious alien. The growing social and economic insecurity and the increased risk of politicization of Muslims issues may cause serious consequences in future.

Low social profile embedded with Muslim religious dogma has augmented the process of gender related discriminations among the households. Status connotes position, category or grading. Status of women in the context of women's access to economic resources, knowledge and political power, as well as their personal autonomy in the process of decision making inside the home and outside in the society is dismal. Muslim culture is rigidly patriarchic and semi-feudalistic. Patriarchy based society and the strict religious dogma of Islam has deteriorated the status of women to a status of second class citizens owing to which women are subordinate to men practically in every aspect of life. Patriarchic norms embedded with male chauvinism have converted Muslim women to the status of *proletariat* and the males as *bourgeoisie.*

The tradition of polygyny practiced by majority Muslim males in this region has sharply deteriorated the position of Muslim women. Polygyny is common in Islam, with the specific limitation that a man can have up to four wives at any one time. The *Quran* clearly states that men who choose this route must deal with their wives justly. If the husband fears that he cannot deal with his wives justly, then he should only marry one. Some Islamic scholars opine that it is mandatory for the husband to tell the first wife if he wants to marry a second one, but her acceptance is not mandatory for him to go through with the subsequent marriage. Women, on the other hand, are only allowed to marry one husband, although they are allowed to remarry after a divorce. Although many Muslim still retain traditional Islamic law which permits polygamy, educated elements within some Muslim society of Miyagaon are challenging the acceptability and practice of polygyny. For many, polygamy is an exception rather than the rule and is traditionally restricted to men who can manage things, and it is illegitimate for a man to marry multiple wives if he is unable to afford to take care of each of them properly However, for the Muslims of Nepal, there is no separate Muslim *Shariat* law, nevertheless the Muslim male are following the polygyny consequently worsening the status of Muslim women.

Despite the dismal condition of Muslim women in Miyagaon, their status is not similar in all groups as women's relative status varies from one ethnic/caste group to another in the whole of Kihun VDC where different caste/ethnic groups live. The status of women in Mongolian communities (Magar ethnic group) generally, is relatively better than that of Dalit and Muslim women. One tangible measure of women's status is their stumpy social status in the lack of private property. Although the constitution offers women equal opportunities, many social, economic, and cultural factors contributed to lower status for girls in Muslims' settlement. Owing to this, women are caught in a *vicious circle* imposed by the norms of patriarchic society. Women have been the victim of prejudice against and insulate far behind as subaltern class, barring a few exceptions, mainly because of long-held orthodox social, cultural, economic structure, Islamic religious doctrine and mind-set of the people of the mainstream Hindu society. Local governments' apathy, the lack of basic infrastructure in indigent marginalized Muslim settlements areas is having a damaging effect. Overpopulation and lack of access to birth control methods drive poverty which is a common phenomenon. The Muslim population is on the rise and it is also veracity that poverty causes overpopulation as it gives women little power to control giving birth, or to have educational attainment or a career. Empowering of women can improve the poverty condition and increase and sustain economic development. When given more rights and opportunities women will begin to receive more education, thus increasing the overall human capital; when given more influence women will proceed more responsibly in helping people in the family or village; and when better educated and more in control of their lives, women will be more successful in bringing down rapid population growth because they have more say in family planning. However, in Muslim settlement no such conditions prevail. Lack of property rights, polygyny, and illiteracy, and backwardness, Islamic religious code of belief embedded with rigid social, cultural and economic structure has seriously restricted women empowerment. Women as marginalized subjugated people can be been taken as *subaltern* people marginalized and dominated.

By and large, for the average Muslims there are many barriers to opportunities. Lack of financial services, as a result of restrictive regulations, such as the requirements for banking licenses, has made it hard for even small micro savings programs to reach the poor. Social-cultural discriminations have negatively impinged on productivity such as stereotyping, gender discrimination, racial and religious discrimination. Modernization theory suggests that cultural values could affect economic success. However, the study on Muslims suggest that values are not as deeply ingrained and that changing economic opportunities explain most of the movement into and out of poverty, as opposed to shifts in values. However, the effects of poverty are long term and are creating a *poverty cycle* operating across multiple levels, from micro to macro--individual, local, national and global.

In contrast to poverty and unemployment which focus on individuals or households, social exclusion is primarily concerned with the relationship between the individual and society, and the dynamics of that relationship. In fact, in many ways, it appears useful to emphasize similarities between the debates about social exclusion and the debates as no societies and groups in the world are entirely inclusive, yet the groups affected and the degree of discrimination varies from one society to another, as do the forms that social exclusion takes. Some forms of discriminations are manifest and deliberate, unofficial, or subtle and unintended. It is the vicious cycle of social exclusion that is responsible for backwardness and poverty of Muslims, leading to higher rates of backwardness and poverty among them. Their productive capacity and poverty reduction rate has been reduced by social exclusion. The development of Muslim community as a whole has been obstructed and the competent operation of market forces has been thwarted that has restrained the economic growth. Discrimination is such traumatic that in the labour market it is making parents decide not meaningful to invest in their children's education. Socially excluded Muslims often do participate, but on unequal terms. Labour markets illustrate this most clearly by exploiting the powerlessness of excluded groups and at the same time reinforcing their disadvantaged position. It is the logic of social exclusion that enlighten why some groups of people remain backward and poorer than others, have less food, die younger, are less economically or politically involved, less educated and are less likely to benefit from services. It is the social exclusion that leads to conflict and insecurity. Excluded groups who are the victim endure from multiple disadvantages that may come together when they have multiple sufferings, unequal rights, denied rights, discriminated and feel marginalized from the mainstream society. Socially excluded people can be an easy victim of discriminations and stereotypical behavior in education. One can see social exclusion among non-disabled groups as socially generated barriers that reduce the ability of the excluded Muslims to interact with mainstream society.

A new dimension to the discussion on social exclusion of hill Muslims of Nepal can be drawn by couching the issue of social exclusion in a rights-based language when we talk about social exclusion as the denial or non-realisation of civil, political, and social rights of citizenship. Such a rights-based approach to the problem of social exclusion has much to recommend. It has great affinity with the capability approach developed by Amartya Sen which calls for efforts to ensure that people have equal access to basic capabilities such as the ability to be healthy, well-fed, housed, integrated into the community, participate in community and public life, and enjoy social bases of self-respect (Sen, 1990). The term social exclusion would be seen as the rejection of the latter three important capabilities.

Educational Tribulations

Education is the illumination of human civilization. The right to education, for example, in a dignified manner reserves a special position, but there prevails different occurrence of discriminations. Children of Muslims areas are getting education but many are deprived of quality education. There is good enrolment of children in school but school dropout is rampant. In the study area, students not going to school are those students who left schools or are school dropouts and some children has not attained the necessary age to attend the school. Some children left their school and are engaged in agricultural works and wage earning. These children cannot attend school due to their parents' poor socio- economic condition, unawareness of parents, inaccessible education system etc.

In Miyagaon settlement, some parents do not send their children to school because education is not positive in favor of them. Other reasons for children not attending school is social hierarchy, gender discrimination and child labor. The *culture of poverty* is also adding to the problem as many of the parents under the grip of culture of poverty are holding the opinion that they are the Muslims and there is no rationality of modern education for them as their destiny is to be subsistence farmers or a laborer in gulf country or India in future, thus there is no utility of education for their children. Rather they prefer Islamic education in *madrassas* that according to them makes easy to be involved with some kind of occupations related to Islamic religion. Those people with modern western education have been trusted less by senior people of Muslim society that is even making the Muslim youths problematic to get a suitable marital candidate for marriage.

There is a high risk of educational underachievement for Muslim children who are from low-income housing circumstances. This often is a process that begins in primary school for some less fortunate children. In the educational system, these children are at a higher risk than other children for retention in their grade, special placements during the school's hours and even not completing their high school education. There are indeed many explanations for why students tend to drop out of school. For children with low resources, the risk factors are similar to excuses such as juvenile delinquency rates and the economic dependency upon their low income parent or parents. Families and society who submit low levels of investment in the education and development of less fortunate children end up with less favorable results for the children. Higher rates of early childbearing in the Muslim community with all the connected risks to family, health and well-being are majorly important issues to address since education from primary to high school are both identifiably meaningful in a life.

Poverty often drastically affects children's success in school. A child's home environment, activities, preferences, mannerisms must align with the broader world and in the cases that they do not these students are at a disadvantage in the school and most importantly the classroom. Therefore, it is safe to state that children who live at or below the poverty level will have far less success educationally than children who live above the poverty line. Poor children have a great deal less healthcare and this ultimately results in many absences from the academic year. Additionally, poor children are much more likely to suffer from hunger, fatigue, irritability, headaches, ear infections, flu, colds and mental problems. These illnesses could potentially restrict a child or student's focus and concentration.

There are many other educational tribulations. Social exclusion of any marginal group is an immense threat for nation building process. Education can play a crucial role in the inclusion of different ethnic and minority group in the main stream of a country. There is the role of education in the social inclusion of Muslims. It is logical to analyze the problems of Muslims of Miyagaon regarding their low literacy based on sociological theory, religious construct and national policies of Nepal on minority. Muslims give high importance to Islamic religious education so they prefer *Madrassas* education than the modern formal education. The schooling of Muslims is low in the locality where religious institutions are not available which is due to the high priority given by Muslim parents to religious education. There is the immediate need of strong policy measure to improve Muslim education in order to enhance their inclusion in development practices and to tackle the menace of raising Islamic fundamentalism in *madrassas*.

There is not a single secondary school in Muslim settlement hence students go to *madrassas* or for formal education at the far distance to *Badharbhanjyang* area which is approximately eight kilometers from Miyagaon, Hukka. Additional predicament is that there is no fixed adult literacy program consequently many adults are illiterate. This education related tribulation makes clear that the prevailing educational system is prone to produce such a manpower in future, which will work in the construction sites and big enterprises of gulf countries. Abiding by the Marxist perspective it is deduced that this tendency will virtually kill the revolutionary sentiment of the Muslims who in the long run will be *alienated* from their family and society and their revolutionary feelings will be killed in the time being.

Stereotype in education is a serious problem. For instance, do students from a certain ethnic or religious groups and so-called low castes have to deal with ethnic stereotypes on a daily basis? While stereotyping in broad-spectrum reflects our expectations and beliefs about the group in question, ethnic stereotypes tend to be negative and prejudicial. Ethnicity may be accredited to, or understood by, individuals; ethnic awareness is not a mechanical subjective correlate of the objective ethnic category. It is notable that religious and ethnic identity may be supposed by others within or outside the group, or forced by foreigners. People are assumed to be members of religious and ethnic groups, not only in fashionable phraseology but also by anthropologists, sociologists and other academics, without careful consideration of the extent to which a religious or ethnic category is actually a group. Fashionable discernment of religion and ethnicity is consistently built upon images constructed up over time, possibly over generations. Many admired views, in the context of Muslims in Hukka, have been inherited through intergenerational socialization processes. Hence, while a religious group could be defined impartially based on certain conventional criteria, it may more precisely symbolize a professed appearance group: a cumulative, category or group of people who are perceived as being distinguishable from a total population because of certain unique characteristics which have high social import for a particular social system. Trendy acumen on religion, ethnicity and ethnic behavior frequently assume the form of stereotypes which is an exaggerated belief associated with some particular category, especially of an ethnic, national, racial or religious minority group. To a substantial degree, ethnic or racial group stereotypes replicate the conventional dealings of perceived appearance groups or racially excluded people.

In Muslim settlement stereotypes in education has been frequently cultured through socialization and armored through social interactions between members of different groups such as *Hindus and Muslims* and *Non-Hindu ethnic groups and Muslims.* Stereotypes is discerned like usually derogatory epithet for religious or ethnic groups, announcement concerning perceived appearance which contain typically depressing emotive meaning, endow with a linguistic gauge of past and present relationships between the object-group and the name-callers. There are many religious jokes prevalent in Kihun, which are told because the teller acknowledges the underlying basis or assumptions about the Muslim religious group or individuals who are the brunt of laughter. Most probably the listener also contributes to these assumptions or the humor would be mislaid. Fabricated stories and publications professing to be non-fiction have consistently denigrated selected Muslim minority religious groups, thereby put in motion the chauvinism of covert or noticeably unreceptive readers. Stereotypes are at hand and affecting students because of the phenomenon of stereotype threat. For example, the popular stereotype prevailing in Nepali society is that *Lahures* (people serving in foreign military services) children are not serious in study, upper caste Hindu Brahmin and Chhetri students are born to be educated and hence are razor-sharp in study, Tarai Madhesi students are deviated but good in mathematics/science, or Muslim and low caste Dalit children are of low strata and hence cannot study, etc. Students will live up or down to perceived expectations of self prophecy. The realities of stereotypes embedded with social constructs about religion cannot be ignored which is a factor responsible for creating the gap between the share of population of Hindu and Muslims in relation to their school going age population and enrollment. This explains why a significant number of children of Muslim children are outside the modern schooling system. The share of enrollment and school attendance of Muslim is lower than their population size. Education of Muslim girls is very meager. Muslim girls' school dropout rate is lofty in all grades. Among multiple reasons, poverty and social discriminations embedded with stereotypes are the major ones.

Muslim settlement is secluded and secondary schools are located far flung and renting the rooms without caste/ethnic/religious based discrimination is difficult. In many cases, teachers from Hindu higher castes preoccupied with stereotypes use and/or pass deprecating remarks or proverbs or examples against Muslims in the class. In schools, Muslim students sit separately on back benches (as they are regarded as untouchables) and also deprived from using educational materials and equipments in many cases. Their participation in sports and extra-curricular activities is very low. Other forms of discriminations are no greeting to Muslim students by Hindu high caste students and disobedience to Muslim teachers by non-Muslim students. Muslim students feel discriminated, depressed, frustrated and terminate schools. Most of Muslim children also give up school as their parents compel them to do household chore, take care of their younger siblings or do wage earning labour.

The issues related to the overrepresentation of some groups such as Hindu Brahmin-Chhetri and underrepresentation of Muslims in education, the state and polity is surfaced heatedly. It is now generally believed that without inclusion in education, it is impossible to accomplish inclusion in other sectors because the credentials provided by education are supposed to level the playing field and make it fair, just and universally acceptable. Once impartiality of opportunity in access and outcome is achieved and institutionalized in education, it may not be essential to have separate provisions for inclusion in the other sectors in societies that believe in and practice genuine meritocracy.

Addictions as a Major Threat

Islam has strictly prohibited the use of liquor and drugs. However, the Muslims of Miyagaon are found to be using liquor and marijuana. Most of the addicts are between 15 to 25 years of age group and children whose fathers are economically backward or whose parents are abroad are mostly involved in these activities. Muslims are involved in diverse professions to make a living but the use of that valuable money for drinking is inviting serious socio-cultural and economic hazards. As alcoholism is against the norms of Islam, the Muslim respondents are reluctant to tell about their addiction habits of liquor consumption. Nevertheless, in this study addictions of all types have been encompassed. The table below presents the involvement of Muslim household heads in different addictions.

Table 5.1

Muslims' in Different addictions

Types of addicts	Number of addicts (Household heads only)	Percent (%)
Smoking cigarettes	24	37.5
Alcohol	2	3.1
Chewing Tobacco	24	37.5
Ganja (Marijuana)	3	4.6
No Addiction	11	17.1
Total	64	100.0

Source: Field Survey, 2012

There are four types of addicts. 24 (37.5%) household respondents are used to smoking, 2 (3.1%) are used to alcohol, 24 (37.5%) are used to tobacco chewing and only 3 (4.5%) respondents are using *Ganja* (marijuana) continuously. 11(17.1%) household heads respondents are not used to any types of addiction. It is comprehensible that majority Muslims are involved in addiction. However, because of strict Islamic traditions which prohibit alcohol, only two households reported of using liquor. Some women Muslims are also used to smoking cigarettes, which may create serious health consequences especially on the part of pregnant women and the baby to be born. In addition, some Muslim males are addict to *marijuana* which is illegal. *Marijuana* addicts are old people who have crossed the age of 65. Some male and female are used to all types of addiction barring *marijuana*. Some Muslims use the tobacco (*Khaini*) which is easily accessible in local market. Addiction is awfully bad habit that can take the life of a person even, but Muslims are used to addict owing to various reasons- owing to companionship, frustration, unemployment, lack of awareness, poverty etc. Owing to fragile social-economic evils based on low agro productions Muslims do daunting work in the day hence they use addiction to forget their fatigueless. In addition, there is no electricity in this part of the country, the Muslims have very limited means of recreation thus they are inclined to addictions of various sorts for recreation and thronging exasperation that is emerging slowly among the Muslims.

Economic Tribulations

The economic problem, occasionally called the fundamental economic problem, is one of the fundamental economic theories in the operation of any economy. It asserts that there is scarcity, that the finite resources available are insufficient to satisfy all human wants. The problem then becomes how to determine what is to be produced and how the factors of production (such as capital and labour) are to be allocated. Economics revolves around methods and possibilities of solving the economic tribulations, however problems remains intact in many cases especially in least developed societies *(en.wikipedia.org/wiki/economic _problem, 2009).* In Miyagaon there prevail countless economic issues. Muslims households possess agricultural land but owing to low productivity, feeding the family members has become a big challenge. For many underprivileged people the subsidiary source of income is labor wages and other lowly paid jobs. Consequently, the resultant problems are low income, malnutrition, poor housing conditions, health, sanitation, poor living standard, debt etc. Owing to the result of stumpy income, they cannot save money for future uses, and therefore their future has no financial security. In addition, people cannot fulfill their basic needs (eating, housing and clothing etc) easily.

Among the 64 households of Muslims with a total population of 466, only 86 (18.45%) people are economically active. With a total population of 466, only 100 people are engaged in different occupations. There are 4 people involved in wage earning labor income and 46 people are having agriculture involvement. The involvement in business is of only 5 people followed by 38 people's involvement in foreign jobs and 6 in teaching field and 1 in government job. It is evident that high percentages of Muslims are involved in agriculture and negligible number of Muslims is involved in government jobs. Muslims generating subsistence income through agriculture works are in majority in Muslims locale. As their educational status is low therefore they cannot do *white-collar jobs* that are why they are engaged in the *blue-collar manual* labour work and subsistence agriculture works. They are trapped in the *culture of poverty* vicious cycle with both types of poverty—*economic and psychological (attitudinal)*. These are the repercussions of underprivileged economic status of Muslims of Miyagaon.

Maximum numbers of houses are of temporary type in the settlement. It is obvious that Muslims economic condition is stumpy and they are facing tribulations owing to low economic status. Many Muslims do not have adequate sanitation because of poverty as well as illiteracy and these may create endemic consequences in future. The widening economic gap between *Have-nots* and *Haves* (both Muslim and non-Muslim) may create serious ramification in future---may be in the form of communal conflicts, scramble for getting more rights and challenging the hegemony of the dominant group. Nevertheless, at the present, the vision of a free and harmonious society gratis of mistreatment seems a distant dream.

Summing up, I argue that *economy* is vital in determining *poverty vs. plenty* statuses. It is the infrastructure or the economic base of society that influences the superstructure or the general character of all other aspects of culture and social structure, such as beliefs, education, religion etc. Consequently, it is construed that there is the fundamental influence of the economy on other areas of society and there exists lofty repercussions of social-economic status including poverty. Muslims are confronting manifold challenges compared to the people of other caste and ethnic groups living in the same village. Hence measured from the relative poverty angle, the Muslims economic tribulations are critical and crucial. Their economic aspects of poverty focus on material needs, typically including the necessities of daily living, such as food, clothing, shelter, or safe drinking water. Their poverty in this sense can be understood as a condition in which a person or community is lacking in the basic needs for a minimum standard of well-being and life, particularly as a result of a persistent lack of income or lacking the knowledge for the better use of the available earnings . The analysis of social aspects of poverty links conditions of scarcity to aspects of the distribution of resources and power in the society and recognizes that poverty is a function of their diminished capability to live the kinds of lives they value. Their social aspects of poverty include lack of access to information, education, health care, or political power.

The Muslims backwardness is understood as an aspect of unequal social status and inequitable social relationships, experienced as social exclusion, dependency, and diminished capacity to participate, victim of Islamic religious credo or to develop meaningful connections with other people in society. Such social exclusion can be minimized through strengthened connections with the mainstream, such as through the provision of relational care to those who are experiencing poverty and marginalization. This study identifies a range of factors which Muslim peoples make out as part of their marginalization and paucity. These include:

- Precarious livelihoods
- Excluded locations/Geographical conditions
- Physical limitations
- Rigid social, cultural and religious structures
- Unequal gender relationships
- Problems in social relationships/Social exclusions
- Lack of security because of the status of religious alien
- Dis-empowering institutions
- Limited capabilities
- Weak community organizations and state apathy
- Bare negligence of their issues by local and national government
- Constitutional barriers, weak policies and legal structures

There are some positive aspects also. Hill Muslims have been influenced heavily by the local Hindu customs. They are surrounded by majority Hindus hence the influence is inevitable. Consequently these Muslims perform less religious activities. Very few *Churoute* in this part of western hills observe *Ramadan* as a month of strict fasting. Despite having different groups of Muslims in Nepal from ethic, linguistic and professional points of view, rigid caste system as prevalent amongst their Hindu neighbors is not practiced by the hill Muslims of Miyagaon. All Muslims perform religious rites jointly in mosques and other places. All Muslims can enter into the mosque and pray sitting side by side. They also eat together during any religious or social gathering. If suitable brides or bridegrooms are found a Muslim of one group does not hesitate to solemnize marriage and there is no social and class stigma attached to it. Usually the hill Muslims of this part used to marry the Muslim girls from Palpa or Lamjung districts of western Nepal. The distinction between Muslims is not rigid for sub-groups. While establishing marital relationships, any Muslim of lower status can make relationship with a higher status Muslim by giving good dowry.

Unlike the Hindus, there is no untouchability prevailing among Muslims. All can dine on one table; they are allowed to change their occupation. They can marry and have good relations with high class after improving their economic conditions. Their worship place is common. They have freedom for change of trade, occupation, craftsmanship etc.

The Muslims in the Kathmandu valley and western Terai region speak Urdu as their mother tongue. These Muslims' Urdu is quite closely related to Hindi. The Western hills' *Churoute* Muslims speak a mixed language of Urdu and Nepali as *'Churoute or Miya Bhasa'* as in Miyagaon, Hukka. Muslims are greatly influenced by the languages spoken in these parts like the Magar ethnic group language. They hardly speak Urdu and speak fluent Nepali.

Churoute were bangle sellers in the past. They were bangle makers also. However, in Miyagaon, Hukka, Muslims have abandoned selling bangles as the vendors of the past. Some Churoute are engaged in cosmetics business and hence sell bangles from shop. This depicts the change in their traditional occupational structure. At the present they have agricultural lands. Many Muslims are agricultural laborers. Some also work as small businessman, farmers, tailors etc and their life is sturdy and tough working. Besides agriculture and business, Muslims are also engaged in various other occupations. Tailors in Nepal are mostly Muslims and low caste Dalit

Hindus. High caste Hindus consider this job as of low excellence. Muslims in Hukka also perform the job of castrating animals like bullocks, buffaloes, goats and horses. Extent of religious inequality within Muslims (between Shia and Sunni sect) in comparison to Hindus or Buddhists is not known here. However, as it appears prime facie, the pecuniary status of the hill Muslims in this part is not satisfactory. As the Muslims are also not rich, the income distribution within the community has also not widened. Rather comparatively, the Muslims are becoming shoddier economically. Muslims though a small minority are not insignificant. They are the third largest religious minority in this village. Though they are not affluent they are contributing to the development of the country as true citizens. Incredibly backward from social and economic point of view, now they are keen advancing slowly to catch up to the mainstream. Improvement of their position in fields of education and economy will strengthen the country itself in the long run.

The quintessence of people's lives is the process of production since for Marxism, human life involves before anything else consumption and ingestion, a habitation, clothing, and many other material things. To meet these necessities of life, production is necessary, but as production satisfies one set of needs, new needs arise and encourage alterations in the ways that productive activity is organized. The elaboration of productive activity creates a division of labor, which, in the end, is alienating because it increasingly divest human of their capacity to determine their productive activities and supports the elites. The track of history right from the development of societies to present involved processes as people vigorously restructure the material conditions of their existence and in the process crisis occurs in the course of demand for more social, economic, political, ethnic and other rights on the part of commoners. With the advent of liberal political environment in the country, the Muslims are also becoming gradually aware and are demanding for more social, economic, political, religious and other rights.

In the analysis of class structure, several early Marxist argued that Marx's scheme had to be revised because there was no real sign of heightened class struggle. A good deal of effort has been expanded in an attempt to adapt the basic idea of a necessary conflict between labor and capital to the conditions of contemporary societies. All these efforts have taken the form of new theories of social class to take account of changes in the patterns of property ownerships changes in relationships at work, class divisions, and rise of elitism and side by side growth of more conscious middle class also, exploitation, growing unrests and the reasons behind conflicts also remaining vital. It is also been widespread realized that it is virtually impossible to comprehend and solve the problems related to backwardness and social unrests in Nepal in the absence of a proper mechanism explaining the relationship between the growing mainstream elitism with its historical legacy and the scramble for more autonomy, social/cultural, economic and political rights on the part of common citizens, ethnic minorities, dalits and religious minorities.

Establishing the correlation between *poverty vs. plenty* dichotomies of *Churoute*, and the conflict perspective, it is evident that Nepalese economy has taken the form of distinctive different capital fractions and of providing an explanation of the monopolies of Hindu upper caste elites. How differences of power develop when elitism is institutionalized, sharing of productive resources to commoners is the issue of special enquiry in the present. Society is chock-a-block of conflicts and harmony, hatred, love, repulsion, attraction owing to growing economic gulf between masses and elites are common. Likewise, conflicts have some social functions and implications, which ought to be seen at – the levels of conflicting parts and at the system as a whole. However, the growing turbulence in various parts of Nepal and untoward incidents (e.g. *rise of culture of fear, religious fundamentalism, regionalism*) etc makes it clear that although social exclusions and inequalities may have functions in creating hierarchies, but when more disproportionate is the hierarchies, the greater is the conflict of interest between dominant and subordinate segments. The more subordinate minority groups become aware of their true collective interests, the more likely are they to question the legitimacy of the existing pattern of social exclusion, inequality and distribution of scarce resources. And this may lead to expressions of sentiments in various forms such as taking the assistance of terrorism, violence, communal riots, mass protests etc. The same may happen in the milieu of the *Churoute* in future. The mushrooming growth of madrassas, growing popularity of Islamic education in madrassas and attraction of poor Muslims to such educations, huge donations received by madrassas from Islamic countries etc are creating alarming situation. As coming events casts their shadows before hence, Nepali policy makers, the government and even the International community need to be alert in time otherwise it will be too late. If *poverty prevails amid plenty* of resources and if the divergences are more sadistic, greater structural alteration will occur and if given a religious and political color, may led to the rise of Islamic fanaticism.

6

SUMMING UP

Guided by the theoretical frame of Marxism, embedded with the notion of Economic Anthropology and Economic Sociology, the qualitative and quantitative facets of Muslims ethnography have been discussed at length. Through a scrutiny of social-ethnographic status of 64 households of Muslims settlements of Miyagaon, Hukka settlement of Kihun VDC of Tanahun, this study explored and derived some lessons and challenges related to social-economic status embedded with Poverty vs. Plenty dichotomies and the consequent implications.

The Muslims settlement of Miyagaon, Hukka is an unplanned settlement, having simple houses and low social-economic profile of the people. It is an irony that though Muslims are bangle seller (*Churoute*) by profession historically, but at the present they are without this profession. Muslim people migrated to Miyagaon, Hukka settlement in the past for selling bangles to Hindu Brahmin, Chhetri women but now there is no tradition of selling bangles. Selling the bangles and cosmetic goods has been Muslims traditional family occupation in the past. Nevertheless, at the present only one old man is practicing the occupation of selling bangles as vendor. The occupational trend is changing. At present most of them are engaged in agricultural activities, working as laborers abroad, exchange and selling the animals (like goat, bull, cows, buffaloes, cow calf's etc), working as teachers, fancy shop business etc. Despite tough agricultural work, agricultural productivity is low. Limited production and traditional agricultural occupation has failed shoddily to fulfill their daily needs consequently leading to the migration of Muslim youths. Till now Muslim economy has been mainly agrarian. Yet this preoccupation with agriculture had missed out quite a number of fundamental characteristics of their household economies. At the micro-level it was totally venetian blind towards diversifications of household employment and income patterns in search for a livelihood. In a household also some members work in agriculture whereas others perform other activities as a labor force in foreign countries. This implies significant amount of remittances crucial for Muslim household economies as well as the national economy.

Social and economic indicators of development determine social-economic status of the people. The social indicators incorporate Family status including the Family Structure, Educational Status, Health/Sanitation, Nutrition, Housing/Shelter, Family Planning, Festivals, and Gender Disparity. In addition, economic indicators are Landholding, Household Income as Agriculture, Employment, Wage labor, Commodities Used.

It is not always very easy to get a just social and economic status in society. Many of ethnic and religious minority groups of Nepal have been categorized as low in terms of religion, ethnicity, culture, gender norms etc. For the Muslims, lack of sufficient food despite the availability of agricultural land, no proper housing, and low standard of living — in general lacking basic needs of human life are the basic features. As they have neither high economically nor higher social status this makes squat the social- economic status, which forces them to remain in hand to mouth conditions forever consequently preparing the ground to face diverse tribulations and bigotry owing to the *vicious cycle* of social-economic backwardness which is far from the hopes of modernization. Social indicators encompassing a wide range of aspects are crucial for generating consequences on development. Measures to indicate social progress, *"social indicators,"* have been conversed in this study, and the importance of economic indicators considered undeniable. Empirical measures of cultural ethnographic states in comparison also remain vital. This study adopted a practical integrated framework combining social and cultural ethnographic indicators of development to measure social and ethnographic status of the Muslims.

Repercussions of the *Poverty vs. Plenty* dichotomies embedded with social-economic status and consequent stipulation the Muslims are confronting at the present are comprehensible. The *economic* dimension of

Muslims relates to the use and insinuation of income, available resources, the competitiveness and the future viability of Muslims family economy and the consequent affliction. Inefficient economic structures, inappropriate expertise as well as the diversity of income sources for households are important rudiments of Muslims' social and economic status.

The *social* dimension relates to questions of opportunities and access to social amenities and services compared to other economic indicators. The issues of equal opportunities and society's ethical standard of behavior can also be considered as embedded to the social dimension. Side by side the Muslims' religious credo, nature of rigid social and cultural ethnographic structure is also the veracities influencing the social and economic status of Muslims in Miyagaon.

The repercussion of Social-economic status and consequent tribulations of Muslims in Miyagaon is **embedded with social-economic status and *poverty* is the prime issue amid the availability of *plenty* of natural resources viz. land, forest etc. Here** poverty is a condition characterized by deprivation of basic human needs, including food, safe drinking water, sanitation facilities, health, shelter, education and information. It depends not only on income but also on access to services. It includes a lack of awareness, adequate income and productive resources to ensure sustainable livelihoods; malnutrition; ill health; limited or lack of access to education and other basic services; increased morbidity and mortality from illness; inadequate housing and sanitation; unsafe environments and social discrimination and exclusion. It is also characterized by lack of participation in decision making and in civil, social and cultural life of the village.

The degrading land resources, depletion of natural resources, backwardness, ignorance and poverty are the ramifications of negligence. Muslims' psychology of feeling insecure surrounded by majority Hindus has created an incongruous psychology of Muslim under which culture of fear and despondency has become a part and parcel of their life. It has created a negative impact, nature and attitudes. Here most people do possess land and forest resources, however their livelihood standard is bleak, houses are crowded and congested. Parents are less aware towards children's education and are unacquainted to the insinuation of education. Despite abundances of resources, many Muslim families are intending to migrate to other areas for a better livelihood. The overall stipulation of the Muslims is fragile which is creating direct implications on their social-economic status which is in turn is creating various sorts of tribulations and consequences. Owing to the limited adoption of modern agricultural technologies the agricultural production has not increased to the extent of eliminating poverty and to enhance their livelihood. Abundances of Chinese cheap consumer goods in the local market have increased the dependency on foreign good which in turn has discouraged and demolished locally made goods and small handicrafts. Rises in the costs of living is making poor peoples livelihood tough. Migration of youths to foreign countries for job has created labor shortage owing to which once the fertile agricultural fields are ghastly converting into barren lands. It is also creating a situation of food shortage owing to which poor Muslims are having insufficient food to consume. Their agricultural production is unable to feed their family throughout the year likewise on the other hand they are unable to spend a greater portion of their budgets on affording food and education of children. Due to the decline of traditional occupation of selling bangles as vendors, Muslims are engaged in cosmetics business and hence sell bangles from shop. This depicts the change in their traditional occupational structure. At the present they have agricultural lands for farming but the production is insufficient to feed all, hence low living style and the poverty is inevitable. Unable to sustain the traditional profession of bangle selling and also the failure to manage effectively the present professions and the income has created a paradox from which the Muslims are unable to get rid of.

Education and healthcare are not reaching the poor Muslims. Due to lack of jobs, unemployed Muslims are forced to migrate to large cities and foreign countries for temporary works. For those unable to find jobs, the consequences are scarcity. Poor health and lack of awareness is severely distressing the productivity at work. Inadequate nutrition in childhood is deflating the ability of individuals to develop their full physical mental capabilities which can seriously hamper the future generation which will consequently exacerbate the process of backwardness and proletariatisation and impoverishment process.

The genesis of social tribulations has to some extent its origin in the family. Majority households have large family structure. Even households having seven members are common. Five and six member households with a large number of children are most common in Muslim settlements.

However, most of these children are lacking proper parental attentions, excellence in education and are even deprived of child rights. In addition, children are obligated to slot in different forms of domestic labor and many susceptible works (e.g. hard work in agricultural fields even at the age of 5 or 6) bearing high hazards. The growing insecurity and the increased risk of politicization of Muslims issues may cause somber consequences in future.

Muslim religious sacrament of regarding family planning as unethical, unholy and anti-Islam has prepared the ground that Muslims are marrying more and more wives (a man marrying even up to five wives) and producing more and more children and rejecting family planning techniques. This is the major reason behind the big family structure of households. The Islamic religious dogma putting a ceiling on family planning, the stress on Muslim women to produce children due to the high social value of children and the way the production of children built into the economic, political and systems of society, has prepared the ground for large size of family and exploitation of women. The crowded housing and illiteracy is the problem for health and sanitation. The easy accessibility of health facilities is also one of the main problems of Muslim settlement. Consequently, the Muslims are unable to raise their status effortlessly, they are becoming *isolated* day by day from the broader society, and a condition of *pauperization* is emerging hence preparing a ground for the conversion of these Muslims into waged people (*proletariat*) under a fast process of *proletariatisation.*

This study has construed that women are partners for sustainable participation and development. They have prominent role to play in livelihood and development along with males but it is not so in authenticity as different sorts of gender inequalities curtail their roles in Muslim society. The status of Muslim women in the context of women's access to economic resources, knowledge and political power, as well as their personal autonomy in the process of decision making inside the home and outside in the society is grim. The condition and position of Muslim women will make sad often times and the Muslim women in the rural areas affected by Maoist insurgents conflict pay the highest price. The gloomy truth is how masculine Muslim societies are making it ever so difficult for women to rise out of the poverty cycle (where the daily struggle is to feed the family for the day) to gain courage to discuss the atrocities they face. Yes, gender related violence is a huge human security threat, how to get around it still thump all efforts thus far. The gap between developed and developing societies in this regard is unplumbed, at least at this point it seems.

Particularly worrisome at a time when there is strong government commitment to incorporate excluded groups into government service, there are the very small percentage of hill Muslims who are well educated. Lack of quality education is veracity. Some students are attending both modern education as well as *madrassas*, the problem for them is to accommodate with both systems of education. There are separate *madrassas* for boys and girls that are against the norms of co-education and it is because of prevailing social hierarchy, ignorance, religious fundamentalism and gender bigotry. The *culture of poverty* is also adding to the problem as it has degraded the attitude of parents. The lack of quality education means that they counter higher barriers in accessing services, taking advantage of economic opportunities – and participating fully as responsible citizens of a democratic state. It also means that they cannot do *white-collar jobs*, are engaged in *blue-collar manual* labour work and subsistence agriculture trapped in the *culture of poverty* cycle that keeps them always in penury.

People of all religions, regions and caste hierarchies, including high caste Hindus in different regions, have been struggling to survive under miserable condition. There is no national religious and ethnic policy in Nepal in the present nor there was in the past but the major issues can be whether Nepal can be a haven of all religions, castes and ethnic groups residing in all regions in a real sense and whether the monopoly (in all sectors) of the few elites from dominant caste groups terminates. In this context, policy should be to accomplish social integration which is a condition of achieving a relatively cohesive and functioning interaction system in a society among different people as a prerequisite to genuine inclusion. National integration is a progressive process of identifying commonalities with respect to common goods but it is imperative to uphold and endorse the distinct religious and ethnic identity of each group through social integration within the framework of the current international political boundaries. To achieve total inclusion, all religious and ethnic groups must have shared values in which the cultural aspirations of each groups are also reflected. But, the practice and implementation is difficult and different than discoursing. Achieving shared values and reflections of cultural aspirations of all groups is immensely difficult in a multicultural and multiethnic country Nepal.

Failure to improve the living standard despite sufficient landholdings and income are the best examples of *poverty amid plenty.* Failure of remittances to bring changes in the overall living condition of their family, are the examples of the vicious cycle of *culture of poverty*. The conformist attitude, *culture of poverty* and stringent Islamic religious credo is generating a dilemma of *poverty amidst plenty* of land and income owing to which Muslims have botched defectively to enhance their status. Primarily, through language, religion and culture, Muslims have been excluded from the mainstream of development. This is what has been customarily continuing. Discrimination occurs in public institutions such as the legal system or education and health services as well as social institutions like the household and in the community. For Muslims, social exclusion is concerned with the inability to participate effectively in economic, social, and cultural life and, in some characteristics, alienation and distance from mainstream society. In contrast to poverty and unemployment which focus on individuals or households, social exclusion of Muslims is primarily concerned with the relationship between the individual and mainstream society, and the dynamics of that relationship. In fact, in many ways, it appears useful to emphasize similarities between the debates about social exclusion and the debates as no societies and groups in the world are entirely inclusive, yet the groups affected and the degree of discrimination varies from one society to another, as do the forms that social exclusion takes. Here some forms of discriminations are manifest and deliberate, unofficial, or subtle and unintended. It is the vicious cycle of social exclusion that causes the poverty of people, leading to higher rates of poverty among affected groups. The productive capacity and poverty reduction rate has been reduced by social exclusion. The development of society as a whole has been obstructed, and the competent operation of market forces disillusioned consequently restraining the economic growth. Discrimination in the context of Muslims is such harrowing that in the labour market it is making parents decide not meaningful to invest in their children's education. Socially excluded groups often do participate but on unequal terms. Labour markets exemplify this most obviously by exploiting the powerlessness of excluded groups and at the same time reinforcing their disadvantaged position. It is the logic of social exclusion that explain to why Muslims remained backward and poorer than others, have low social standards, consume less nutritious food, die younger, are less economically or politically involved, less educated and are less likely to benefit from services. It is the social exclusion that leads to conflict and insecurity. As excluded groups Muslims, who are the victim endure from multiple disadvantages that may come together when they have manifold sufferings, unequal rights, shorn of rights, show favoritism and feel marginalized from the mainstream society. As socially excluded they can be an easy victim of discriminations and stereotypical behavior in the matters of religion and politics.

Preponderance Muslims are not involved in any profitable or industrial goings-on, and the best parts of them are either unskilled laborers or small-scale subsistence farmers, with a bit of some lower-level civil servants. Ignorance and backwardness are unbridled, and this has led to their forfeiture of their human rights. Even in the Islamic belief that they profess their knowledge of Islamic principles and culture is very insufficient and may be easily manipulated of their neophyte sentiments by the radical Islamic. The main reason behind this is the lacking and backwardness in modern education and their high priority to *madrassas*. Hence, the solution is only to establish such institution privately to conduct the educational activities which would work for the production of well educated, skilled personnel and professionals having spirits of modern Islam. Government negligence of *madrassas* will boost up the evil desires of fundamentalist section of Muslim community. Muslims will continue to be beleaguered if government authorities continue to create obstacles during the registration and issuance of citizen certificates or the certificates related to the *madrassas* registration. *Madrassas* are running out of economic and human resources, quality and are focusing more on Islamic orthodoxy which may generate serious quandary in future. Nepalese Government has failed to bring any assisting programs to flourish such *madrassas* whose financial condition remains always vulnerable and thus there is a need of bringing special programs to uplift the situation and quality of education are being given in such *madrassas*. Muslims are not capable of combating their backwardness in social, economic, and political matters, nor are they capable of confronting the anti-Islamic activities and their enticements hence social exclusion has become a part of their life. **The sectors of varied forms of exclusion of Muslims** are as follows:

1. Educational Sector

Hindu teachers, higher castes, in many cases, preoccupied with stereotypes pass insulting remarks or proverbs or examples against Muslims in the class. Muslim students sit separately on back benches (as they are regarded as untouchables) and also deprived from using educational materials and equipments in many cases. Muslim students' participation in sports and extra-curricular activities is very low. Muslim students feel discriminated, depressed, frustrated and terminate schools. The issues related to the overrepresentation of Hindu high caste students and underrepresentation of Muslims in education, the state and polity is surfaced intensely. Without inclusion in education, it is impossible to accomplish inclusion in other sectors because the credentials provided by education are supposed to level the playing field and make it fair, just and universally up to standard. The gravest situation of Muslim has been understood as backwardness in education. And the reason behind the illiteracy is poverty and lack of proper awareness towards the education though Islam has made it compulsory for every Muslim men and women to get education. Most of them are leading the life under extreme paucity and below the poverty line. The possibility of Muslims getting higher education is very fewer.

2. Constitutional and Legal Sector

Muslims are the victims of social exclusion. All the constitutions of Nepal developed and modified up to now have failed to provide acceptance to the Muslim communities. And this is the main important reason of the exclusion that Muslims were out of enjoying the constitutional and legal rights.

3. Political Sector

Muslim communities are and were used just as the vote bank by the political parties of Nepal. They understood and raised the problems of Muslim communities rightly during the time of election but sided back just after entertaining the hunger of vote. Not a single party has raised the issues of Muslims either in the assembly or cabinet and thus Muslim are the victims of seclusion and deprived of serving the nation politically and in administration sectors. There are no fixed seats for the Muslim candidates in the political system.

4. Economic and Employment Sector

Muslims are deprived from the work in Nepali army and administration, but a very few number of Muslims are in government jobs. And this is the reason of negative affect and obstruction in progress. And it has diminished the self confidence of the Muslims.

5. Gender Discrimination

Muslim female are socially, culturally, legally, politically, economically and gender wise very backward. Islamic traditions have seriously deteriorated the status of Muslim women.

Summing up, in broad-spectrum, the Muslims marginalization and backwardness is understood as an aspect of unequal social status and inequitable social relationships, experienced as social exclusion, dependency, and diminished capacity to participate, or to develop meaningful connections with other people of mainstream society. Such social exclusion can be minimized through strengthened connections with the mainstream, such as through the stipulation of associative heed to those who experience social exclusion, poverty and backwardness.

Despite the tribulations embedded with social and economic status, the religious practice of the Muslim settlement is simple. Mosques are located in those areas which are easily accessible to all. It shows that though underprivileged socially and economically, Muslims are practicing their own faith amid paucity and insecurity. Majority of the Muslim people rejoice festivals in simple manner but with religious *gaiety, pomp and merry*. Despite social exclusion Muslims have very good and cordial relationship with their Hindus neighbors who observe Hindu festivals like Durga puja, Deepawali, Krishna janmastami etc. A proper religious syncretism exists between Hindus and Muslims. The Muslims use to invite their Hindu neighbors during marriage ceremonies. In such cases the food are cooked by Hindu Brahmin and all the Hindu and ethnic groups' invitees eat the food. Likewise, in the case of the marriages and other ceremonies of Hindus and Buddhists, the Muslims are invited and they are fed foods cooked by Hindu Brahmins. They are helpful to each other at the time of need and there have been no religious conflicts and rows so far.

I argue that in Nepal an understanding of social-cultural, religious and ethnic dimensions is essential to the development of inclusive policies and programs that respond more effectively to the legitimate needs and demands of Nepal's diverse population including the religious minorities. It is of the essence to understand the process of understanding and responding to Nepal's diversity by carrying out an examination through the lens of ethnicity/caste, religion, and regional identity. This will potentially help in understanding the sentiments of the minority groups which will consequently reduce the possible tensions and conflicts in future. However, in the context of Muslims the cultural concept of being religious alien, culture of poverty and stringent Islamic religious doctrine has crafted a paradoxical condition. Cultural values are not as intensely inbuilt and that altering economic opportunities can explicate most of the movement into and out of backwardness and poverty, as opposed to shifts in values. However, the effects of social exclusion and backwardness are creating a *poverty cycle* operating across multiple levels, individual, local, national and global. The culture of poverty and superstitious doctrines are crafting a dilemma *of poverty amidst plenty* of human resources, land and income and the Muslims have failed badly to escape from backwardness. Their illiteracy, poverty and low social status signifies that they face higher barriers in accessing services, taking advantage of economic opportunities – and participating fully as responsible citizens of a democratic state and continued to be excluded from the management and decision making processes at different levels. Such exclusion ultimately cost high for the society as Muslim folks are loosing interest in legal systems, administrative systems, health/education etc. The lack of adequate inclusion of these populations in institutional stake has helped maintain the gap between people, the institutions and mainstream. Consequently, poverty and vulnerability has continued to transmit through generations among the Muslims. Consequently the hopes of modernization has been restrained under the vicious cycle of social-economic chauvinism, failure to raise social-economic status has led to isolation from the mainstream society, and a condition of pauperization is emerging preparing a ground for the conversion of Muslims into waged laborers (proletariat).

Hidden assumptions of culture and religion are embedded in culture and cultural discourses and various institutions, the important thing are to use the lenses of culture to comprehend this. Unless one comprehends hidden assumptions of cultural significance through cultural lenses it seems difficult to think about development. These hidden assumptions determine how local people perceive their natural and human resources, manage and control in the long run. Such lenses are relatively easy to see in relation to gender as seen from the present study where it has been traced that gender relations are very vital in determining the status of the people. The failure to consider gender differences/inequalities may results in *fiasco*, and the doomed failure of all development efforts to upgrade the social-economic status of women as well man. It is also inferred that social and economic analysis is incomplete without an understanding of cultural ethnographic and religion based gender differences and religious inequalities as Muslims who are generally seen more as *religious alien* than as a group of people who are diffident with stumpy social-economic status.

Powerlessness has increased among the Muslims. Hence, it is a veracity that the increasing gap in status between the poor Muslims living in Muslims settlement and the people from the mainstream society need to be paid due attention.

This study has deduced that the more imbalanced the development efforts especially *Mainstream versus Muslims settlement and* allotment of scarce resources, state apathy, the wider will be the inconsistency of interest between foremost and secondary segments for obtaining the power, possessions and resources and more the sentiment and grievances are ignored, more stress and extremism will be created in the society. Proper *understanding the sentiments of the religious minorities will consequently lessen the possible tensions and ethno-religious conflicts in the region.* If people become aware of their factual combined interests, the more likely are they to defy the validity of the existing pattern of exclusions. If the sentiment of minorities is overlooked, there may be more apathy, hostility and trauma in the process of inclusive democratic *(called Loktantrik Samabesi in Nepali)* process. Lopsided distribution of resources, existing discriminations, social exclusion, and centralization of political power and centuries old feudalistic design amidst the mishandling of the rhetoric of *Samabesi* (inclusiveness) can lead to the rise of more crisis and instability. Increasing number of religious organizations is the evidence. This may create serious troubles in future. The relationship between religious politics and representative inclusive democracy presents a dilemma for scholars and policy makers, however all religious organizations may not be adversative to democracy and that democratization with commitment can proceed in diverse and unpredicted ways by integrating diverse ethnicities, religions, class, cultural, societal, historical and geopolitical realities . However, that requires development of the feeling of inclusion, leadership, self-confidence and capacity development on the part of marginalized groups to lead other caste, ethnic and religious groups and a change in the stereotypical thinking of dominant groups. One of the major demands of the Nepali people's political movement 2006 was not just democracy and republic, but more *inclusive* democracy and greater government attention to overcoming the persistent disparities between the dominant high caste hill dwellers (*Parbatiyas)* the non-hill dwellers (*non-parbatiyas including the Madhesi and Muslims)*, Hindus and Non-Hindus, Castes and Ethnicities.

Human well-being has many dimensions and thus, measuring concepts like *poverty* or *social exclusion* or *plenty* requires data from many aspects of people's lives. A number of works have explored gender, caste/ethnic, religious and regional disparities in poverty and human development outcomes in Nepal, but has not been sensibly useful in bringing any changes in people's lives. The same tendency prevails in the case of the hill Muslims. Many researches have been conducted on them by both native and foreign researchers using both *emic* and *etic* approaches, but all has been *paper tigers* and there have been fewer utilities of all the findings. Muslims are the citizens of Nepal and their sensitivity is Nepali however they have been deprived of many rights because of their religious faith. They have been the *dumb children of Nepal.* The social-ethnographic status of the Muslims of Miyagaon as extremely low, full of tribulations and depressing amid plenty of natural resources such as land and forest and income owing to ineptitude, lack of responsiveness and powerlessness. As such for the amelioration of problems, this study suggests few suggestions, which if implemented by Nepalese policy makers and the concerned stakeholders (including the donors), may bring alteration and may avert probable future inconsistencies and religious extremism.

1. Old laws and policies ought to be made more flexible and new policies devised at the National and local levels to make social inclusion more pragmatic and sensible.
2. Policies need to be devised to mobilize the locally available natural resources including the land, forest and water resources.
3. To reduce economic disparity, employment should be generated. Employment is also essential to raise the status of lower economic groups Muslims. Policy of giving *'training of fishing rather than giving a fish to unemployed'* should be adopted. Investment should be targeted to build infrastructure of rural sector by enhancing the agro sector.
4. Nepal's progress as an inclusive state – may require *more effort and investment per person* than the groups that have been reached so far. This is especially true for women who face multiple exclusions having consistently low indicators.
5. Muslims are the minority groups of South Asia especially Nepal and India. Rise of Islamic fundamentalism because of social exclusion and frustrations may create long term effects on the security situation of the whole region. Hence, the issues and concerns of Muslims should be discussed at micro to macro (local

to national levels, national to international) to draw attention of all the concerned individuals/institutions/donors/governments whose policies, programs and actions are likely or are to be linked to the Muslims.

6. A phenomenon of economic equity and social justice should be the underlying principle, while addressing Muslims' issues.
7. Attempts need to be made from the Muslim community to get rid of the *culture of poverty* by making structural social-cultural reforms and enhancing the quality of education.
8. Serious thought needs to be made on how to increase hill Muslims exposure to various forms of media so they can become active and empowered citizens and get rid of the vicious cycle of social exclusion and *culture of poverty*.

Blanket programs designed in Kathmandu will not work for all groups. Programs need to be designed based on deeper knowledge of the local needs and conditions of different groups – and as far as possible in consultation with them.

Health and population communication programs are necessary and

- It is necessary to design messages in local languages
- Encourage front line workers, who are from the local community, speak the local language and know the local norms, religious values and concerns
- There is no fixed adult literacy program for women in Muslims area. Adult literacy program for women is most important because it will enhance their social-economic status and their knowledge about family planning. Adult education can make the people aware about the menace of religious fundamentalism and protect them from being manipulated easily by the vested interests of radical Islamic groups.
- In the current context of state restructuring in Nepal special efforts need to be made by the Election Commission, political parties and NGOs to reach minority groups with the information that they need to participate meaningfully in the process of mainstream.

References

Barnard, Andy, Burgess, Terry and Kirby, Mike (2004). Sociology. United Kingdom: Cambridge University Press.

Beall, Jo and Piron, Laure-Hélène. (2005) *Social Exclusion Review*. London School of Economics Overseas Development Institute.

Bicker, Alan, Pottier, Johan, Sillitoe, Paul Ed. (2002). Participating Development Approaches to Indigenous Knowledge. London: Routledge.

Bista, Dor B (1967) . People of Nepal. Kathmandu, Ratna Pustak Bhandar.

Bourdieu, Pierre and Loïc J.D. Wacquan (1992). *An Invitation to Reflexive Sociology*. Oxford: Polity Press.

Central Bureau of Statistics. *Population Statistics of Nepal. National Population and Housing Census 2011,* Kathmandu.

___________ (2011) *Population Census 2011,* National Report, Central Bureau of Statistics, National Planning Commission Secretariat in collaboration with UNFPA and HMG/Nepal.

___________ (2011) *Population of Nepal,* Population Census 2011, selected tables on Caste/Ethnicity, Mother Tongue and Religion, Central Bureau of Statistics, National Planning Commission Secretariat in collaboration with UNFPA and HMG/Nepal.

___________ (2011*) Population Monograph of Nepal.* Central Bureau of Statistics Ramshah Path, Katmandu, Nepal.

Cairns, D (2007). *The Study of population an account and Appraisal.* Chicago University press.

Coser, Lewis A. (1967). *Continuities in the Study of Social Conflict,* New York. Free press and London: Collier Macmillan.

Dobbin, Frank, (2004) *The New Economic Sociology.* Princeton University Press.

Duffy K. (1995) *Social Exclusion and Human Dignity in Europe.* Council of Europe.

Gaborieau, Marc (2001) In 'Muslim community of South Asia', Edited by T.N. Madan, Manohar. Delhi University Press.

Giddens, Anthony (2001): *Sociology.* 4th edition. New York: Karean Birdsall.

Helpton, John (2005) A History of Nepal. U.K. Cambridge University Press.

International Encyclopedia of Sociology (2003). Volume I, New Delhi: Bhavana Books and Prints.

Magill, Frank N. (2003) *International Encyclopedia of Sociology,* Volume I, New Delhi, Bhavana Books and Prints.

Marx, Karl and Engles, Fredrich (1963). *The Communist Manifesto,* of Karl Marx and Fredrich Engles. In D.Rayzanoff. (Ed.) London.

Mathur, Hari Mohan (1996) Anthropology and development in traditional societies. Vikas Publishing House Pvt. Ltd.India.

Nepal District Profile (2011). Nepal Development Information Institute, Kathmandu.

NPC (National Planning Commission). (2008) Government of Nepal, Kathmandu.

Rao, C.N. Shankar (2002). *Sociology Primacy Principles.* Delhi: S. Chand and Company Ltd.

Scott P. William (1999). *Dictionary of Sociology. New Delhi:* Goyal Saab Publishers and Distributors, for the Indian Edition.

Sen, Amartya. (1990). *Justice: Means versus Freedoms.* Philosophy and Public Affairs.

Turner H. Jonathan (1999). *The Structure of Sociological Theory.* Jaipur India: Rawat Publication.

Upadhyay, Prakash (2007). *User group's participation in community forest resources management in western Nepal*, Unpublished PhD dissertation in Anthropology, Tribhuvan University, Kirtipur, Nepal.

Yogindar, Sikand (2004). *Muslims in India since 1947: Islamic Perspectives on Inter-faith*. Oxford Press.

Websites

*(en.wikipedia.org/wiki/**economic problem, 2009)***

(*en.wikipedia.org/wiki/Social_status.2007*).

Appendix I

Key Questions Considered for Interview

1. General Background Date ....
   Name of Respondent ....
   Age .... Gender ....
   Ethnicity .... Occupation ....
   Education .... Religion ....
   Marital Status ....
2. Where are they (hill Muslims) from? When and why did they migrate to this area of Nepal and when?

   ....

   ....
3. Description of the Family Members:
4. Qualifications of the family members: Household Head ....
   Members qualifications

   ....

   ....
5. Distance of primary school from home ....
   Where do children go for higher study?

   ....

6. Are you (Household heads only) given elderly education nearby?

   a. Yes b. No

7. Are you (Household heads only) given any facilities for education by any agencies?

   a. Yes b. No

8. Were you discriminated in the name of son or daughter for education?

   ....

   ....

   Have you ever discussed your children's education with school teacher?

   a. Yes b. No

9. What is your concept on health and health status?

   ....

10. Do you check your health regularly?

    a. Yes b. No

11. What type of health services is available here?

    ....

12. Where do you go for health check up?

    a) Health post b) Hospital

    c) Traditional healer d) Private clinic

13. Do you immunize your children?

    a. Yes b. No

14. When have they been immunized?

    a. Sometimes b. Changed Weather

    c. Usually d. Never

15. Have you done family planning? If yes what type? Temporary or permanent?

    a. Yes b. No

    ....

16. Which type of toilet do you have?
    a. Permanent b. Temporary
    c. Pit Only d. No
17. Do you care your and children's personal hygiene and clean dress?
    a. Yes b. No
18. What is the source of drinking water?
    a) Tube well b) Piped water
    c) Water spring d) River
19. Are you satisfied with the availability of drinking water facilities?
    a. Yes b. No
20. What are your major festivals?

    ....

    ....
21. How do you celebrate your festivals?
    a) Simply b) Lavishly
22. Do you have temple/ mosque/ monastery nearby?
    a. Yes b. No
23. Do you believe the supernatural powers?
    a. Yes b. No
24. Do you have any Procession in your community?
    a. Yes b. No
25. Are there any conflicts in your society in the name of religion, festivals and caste/ethnicity?
    a. Yes b. No
26. Have you been discriminated in the name of religion?
    a. Yes b. No

    How ....
27. If yes, what sorts of discriminations? Please mention.

    ....

    ....

28. Are you satisfied with the prevailing development condition of your village?

    a. Yes b. No.

    c. No idea

29. Compared to the past, in the present there has been change in the infrastructure development in your community or not ?

    If yes what sort of ?

    ....

    why?

    ....

    If no what sort of ?

    ....

    why?

    ....

30. What is their existing trend of social-economic and ethnographic stipulation and characteristics?

    ....

    ....

31. And how they subsist and what are their livelihood patterns, conventions, and effects of modernization?

    ....

    ....

32. What type of physical facilities is available in your home?

    a. Toilet b. Water taps

    c. Electricity d. Telephone/mobile

    e. Cupboard f. Bicycle

33. Which type of communication media are at home?

    a. Radio b. TV.

    c. V.C.D /D.V.D. d. Computer

34. What type of social exclusions, difficulties and tribulations are you facing here?

    a. Social b. Economic

c. Cultural d. Political

e. Others

35. What is the source of your household income?

a. Agriculture b. Service

c. Business d. Labor hood

e. Pension f. Others

36. What is your current occupation?

a. Agriculture b. Service

c. Business d. Labor hood

e. Pension f. Others

37. How many members of your family are engaged in economically income generating activities?

a. 1 b. 2

c. 3 d. 4 and Above

38. What is the average income of your family?

a. Less than 2000 b. 2000-4000

c. 4000- 8000 d. 8000 and above

39. How much money is spent in a month for maintaining your family?

....

....

40. You receive goods from relatives or not?

a. Yes b. No

41. What is the position of females in your family at decision making?

a. No role b. Partial

c. Advisory d. Absolute

42. What is your land holding portion here?

....

43. What is the type of your house? What type of house do you have?

a. Permanent b. Temporary

44. How many rooms are there in your house?

    a. Single b Double

    c. Three d. Four and above

45. Have you borrowed loan from any institution? If yes, for what purpose?

    ....

    ....

    Name of institution ....

46. Are here any INGO, NGO, agencies or government involved in your economic support here?

    If yes which? ....

47. Do you know about nutrition?

    a. Yes b. No

48. Do you eat nutritious food?

    a. Yes b. No

49. How many times do you give food to children?

    ....

50. What may be the economic implications on health status?

    ....

    ....

51. Do you drink alcohol during the festivals celebration?

    a. Yes b. No

52. In general, what are the repercussions of social-economic status and tribulations?

    ....

    ....

53. In your view prosperity (plenty) has increased or decreased in your family?

    If yes, what are the reasons?

    ....

    If no, what are the reasons?

    ....

54. Prosperity (plenty) has increased or decreased in your village?

    If yes, what are the reasons?

    ....

    If no, what are the reasons?

    ....

55. What is the role of social exclusion and culture of poverty in contributing to prosperity and poverty of the people? Please mention in brief.

    ....

    ....

    ....

    ....

56. In the past life was simple or is at the present?

    ....

    Why? Write reasons

    ....

    ....

57. How are development, political structure, state policies and apathy, ethnography embedded conventions and social/cultural structure in rural Nepal organized and what influences they wield over their traditions, renovations and development efforts?

    ....

    ....

    ....

    ....

58. Any suggestion

    ....

    ....

Appendix II

KEY INFORMANTS INTERVIEW

1. Brief description of the settlement.
2. Main Identity of this area.
3. Composition of the settlement by sex, caste, religion, age, marital status, literacy rate, economic status, ethnicity etc.
4. Issues related to participation of all sections –elite, caste, ethnic and religious groups, in social and development work of this area.
5. Muslim women's participation in development activities of this settlement.
6. Differences of life standard between rich and poor. Managerial difficulties faced during the past, solutions and the present resolutions for improvements.
7. Linkages with any organization, which are prone to improve daily life. Role of local and national government and NGO officials in the local people's struggle for existence.
8. Land ownership certificate and struggle for getting the ownership, citizenship certificate and other state benefits.
9. Support of VDC ward office at this settlement. Activities and works accomplished by ward offices. Motivational steps taken by wards and DDC to boost the moral of Muslims.
10. Important person supporting to this area for development.
11. Attempts to improvements --socially, culturally, economically and politically.

12. Implications of social-economic and ethnographic status.
13. Problems related to settlement and other facilities allied to infrastructure development --schools, drinking water, health etc.
14. Persuasion of female members, disadvantaged groups, youths and teenagers to participate in development activities of this region.
15. There is *plenty or poverty* in village.
16. Resource utilization pattern in village.
17. Relationship of Muslims with others --Hindus, ethnic groups etc.
18. Social exclusions, discriminations, conflict issues cases and types.
19. Relationship issues.
20. Religious Conflicts
21. Suggestions for betterment and amelioration.

Appendix III

MAP 1

Tanahun District in the Map of Nepal

Source: District Development Committee, Tanahun, 2012

Appendix IV

MAP 2

Map of Tanahun District Showing Kihun VDC

Source: District Development Committee (DDC), Tanahun, 2012

INDEX